ObamaCare Simplified

Your Go-to Guide for
Understanding ObamaCare

HAMISU SALIHU, MD, PHD

WESTBOW
PRESS
A DIVISION OF THOMAS NELSON
& ZONDERVAN

Copyright © 2014 Hamisu Salihu, MD, PhD.

All rights reserved. No part of this book may be used or reproduced by any means, graphic, electronic, or mechanical, including photocopying, recording, taping or by any information storage retrieval system without the written permission of the publisher except in the case of brief quotations embodied in critical articles and reviews.

WestBow Press books may be ordered through booksellers or by contacting:

WestBow Press
A Division of Thomas Nelson & Zondervan
1663 Liberty Drive
Bloomington, IN 47403
www.westbowpress.com
1 (866) 928-1240

Because of the dynamic nature of the Internet, any web addresses or links contained in this book may have changed since publication and may no longer be valid. The views expressed in this work are solely those of the author and do not necessarily reflect the views of the publisher, and the publisher hereby disclaims any responsibility for them.

Any people depicted in stock imagery provided by Thinkstock are models, and such images are being used for illustrative purposes only. Certain stock imagery © Thinkstock.

ISBN: 978-1-4908-5768-8 (sc)
ISBN: 978-1-4908-5770-1 (hc)
ISBN: 978-1-4908-5769-5 (e)

Library of Congress Control Number: 2014919138

Printed in the United States of America.

WestBow Press rev. date: 10/24/2014

CONTENTS

Preface vii

Chapter 1   What Is ObamaCare? 1

Chapter 2   ObamaCare Health Exchange Basics 17

Chapter 3   Pregnant Women, Illegal Immigrants,
            Medicaid and Medicare under ObamaCare 37

Chapter 4   Dental and Eye Care under ObamaCare: Part 1 56

Chapter 5   Dental and Eye Care under ObamaCare: Part 2 71

Chapter 6   ObamaCare: Opposing Viewpoints 87

Chapter 7   ObamaCare and the Business Environment 103

Chapter 8   How the Health Exchange Works 114

Chapter 9   How Does ObamaCare Affect Me? 128

Chapter 10 ObamaCare as It Unfolds 141

Chapter 11 ObamaCare Literacy in Medical Technology 154

PREFACE

The Patient Protection and Affordable Care Act of 2010—ObamaCare—has sparked great relief among those who previously had limited options for health care coverage while creating apprehension among those who resent a law requiring insurance for all. Intense debate continues regarding the impact this law will have on Americans and this great nation. The long-term outcome of ObamaCare remains to be seen, but all of us need to understand this law and how it may affect our lives. This book does not weigh in on the ObamaCare debate; instead, it provides a user-friendly approach to understanding the basic tenets of the law, with questions and responses concerning coverage and scenarios to aid comprehension.

ObamaCare Simplified also deals with issues that are not often discussed but should be. Chapter 6, for instance, addresses common misconceptions about the law and provides factual information that will allow readers to draw their own conclusions. This book will allow readers to contribute to the ObamaCare dialogue regardless of their position on the issue.

As a board-certified physician and a public health professional, I am adamant about offering my patients health care information they can understand and use. I encourage them to ask questions, and I try my best to give them honest and unbiased answers. This book follows the same principle, building on fundamental knowledge to empower the consumer whether an individual, a small business, or a large corporation. The material will enable readers to take advantage of ObamaCare's benefits, such as subsidies and tax credits, and to avoid its pitfalls.

Topics extend from the general, including ObamaCare basics, to the specific, such as vision and dental coverage and health insurance for special populations. I have dedicated the final chapter to literacy in medical technology, an area poorly understood by most of us because we are intimidated by the topic. This is mostly because we lack a basic understanding of the technology and feel overwhelmed by its complexity. Since medical technology accounts for a significant portion of health care advancement and expenditure, grasping what it is and how it will affect our lives under ObamaCare is imperative. This book will not make everyone technologically literate, but it will set the foundation for continuing study.

This book's versatility makes it useful in a variety of settings. For example, it could be used as a textbook in medical, business, health policy, and public health courses. *ObamaCare Simplified* can easily be read cover to cover, and each chapter can stand alone as a topic for discussion. The book can be a valuable employee training manual in small businesses or large corporations. The straightforward dialogue makes this book an ideal addition to any coffee table, bookshelf, and personal or public library. It is a practical tool for learning the basics of ObamaCare and the impact it will have on us as individuals and as a nation.

CHAPTER 1

What Is ObamaCare?

Introduction to the chapter: ObamaCare regulates health insurance coverage. Although the law has received wide media coverage, a majority of citizens still do not understand its basic tenets. This chapter and the ones that follow will simplify the main provisions of ObamaCare in a question-and-answer format, using scenarios to reinforce understanding.

Objective of the chapter: This chapter will enable readers to understand the components of ObamaCare, including universal coverage and affordability, qualification criteria for tax credits, and essential health benefits. The regulations regarding the mandate and pre-existing conditions will be explained with easy-to-understand scenarios that clarify complex issues.

1. Sue, who is nineteen and leaving for college, receives a health insurance application from the school. She doesn't know whether to fill it out. She is on her parents' health plan. Can she remain on that plan and ignore the school's application?

    a. No, because ObamaCare stipulates that as soon as a child turns eighteen, he or she must be on a separate health plan.
    b. Yes, because ObamaCare stipulates that a child may stay on his or her parents' health plan until age twenty-one.

c. Yes, because ObamaCare allows a child to remain on his or her parents' health plan until age twenty-six.
d. All of the above are irrelevant because she is now in college.

2. Sam, the owner of a small business, does not have health insurance. He weighs the pros and cons of purchasing insurance and decides that, since he is healthy, he is not going to worry about it. Which of the following could happen under the law?

   a. He will be fined 5 percent of his monthly income until he purchases a health insurance policy.
   b. He will be ordered by a court to purchase health insurance.
   c. The federal government will provide him with Medicaid coverage until he makes a decision.
   d. He will be charged a penalty and will have to pay for all of his health care.

3. Sam is considering purchasing a health insurance policy after being diagnosed with gastro- esophageal reflux disease. Which of the following could happen under the law?

   a. He will be charged a higher premium for having a pre-existing health condition.
   b. The insurance company may refuse him coverage.
   c. He will not be charged a higher premium, but he will receive less coverage than someone without a pre-existing health condition.
   d. He will be able to purchase a health plan without any of the complications listed above.

4. ObamaCare stipulates which of the following?

   I. Universal health coverage
   II. Children can be on their parents' policy until twenty-one years of age.

III. Health insurance carriers cannot deny coverage.
IV. Carriers cannot charge more for pre-existing conditions.

   a. I, III, IV
   b. I, II, III
   c. I, II, IV
   d. All of the choices above

5. What is ObamaCare's official name?

   a. Patient Protection and Affordable Care Act
   b. Healthcare and Education Reconciliation Act
   c. Health Aid and Patient Responsibility Act
   d. America's Affordable Health Choices Act

6. Health care involves both mental and physical health. Given this fact, if a patient with health insurance walks into a clinic and her primary concern is anxiety due to stress, which of the following scenarios is unlikely?

   a. The staff will ask the patient to sign in and will check her coverage.
   b. The staff will not provide assistance because stress is not considered a legitimate health concern.
   c. The doctor will prescribe medication if appropriate.
   d. The patient will be referred to a psychiatric office for further diagnosis if needed.

7. Which of the following best describes the operation of the Small Business Health Options Program (SHOP)?

   a. As of 2014, until December 2015, only businesses with fewer than fifty full-time equivalent employees are eligible.
   b. If a business is determined to be eligible, the owner and spouse can also sign up for SHOP.

c. As of 2014, under ObamaCare a small business is one with fifty or fewer full-time employees.
   d. All of the above

8. Which of the following are the goals of ObamaCare?

   I. Universal health coverage
   II. Creating a source of revenue for the government
   III. Making health care more affordable for those who cannot otherwise afford it
   IV. Balancing pay among health care professionals

   a. I, II, III
   b. I, II, IV
   c. I, III, IV
   d. None of the above

9. The launch of ObamaCare heralds a new era in health insurance, with many more changes to be made until 2022. One of the most important stipulations is that individuals must be covered under what kinds of health plans?

   a. Private, state, or federally assisted providers
   b. Private or state providers because the federal government will no longer be providing assistance.
   c. Only federally assisted providers
   d. Only private providers

10. President Obama aims to redirect money in a way that helps the common man. ObamaCare is one of the means through which he plans on accomplishing this. Right now, many Americans are without

health insurance. As of July 2013, how many Americans were without health coverage?

a. Twelve million
b. Forty-four million
c. Seventy-six million
d. Ninety-eight million

ObamaCare: Affordability and Essential Health Benefits Forty-Eight Contiguous States and Washington, D.C.

Note: The 100 percent column shows the federal poverty level for each family size, and the percentage columns that follow represent income levels commonly used as guidelines for health programs.

Household Size	100%	133%	150%	200%	300%	400%
1	$11,490	$15,282	$17,235	$22,980	$34,470	$45,960
2	15,510	20,628	23,265	31,020	46,530	62,040
3	19,530	25,975	29,295	39,060	58,590	78,120
4	23,550	31,322	35,325	47,100	70,650	94,200
5	27,570	36,668	41,355	55,140	82,710	110,280
6	31,590	42,015	47,385	63,180	94,770	126,360
For each additional person, add	$4,020	$5,347	$6,030	$8,040	$12,060	$16,080

http://aspe.hhs.gov/poverty/13poverty.cfm

11. Sara is a mother of three, and her husband is terminally ill. He is indefinitely hospitalized, and she makes $70,000 a year as a dental hygienist. Where do her household size and total income put her on the chart for poverty level?

a. 150%
b. 200%

c. 250%
d. 300%

12. Peter is a mechanic and has a health plan through his company. He has a wife, two daughters, and a son. Given that his wife makes $35,000 a year as a teacher, what is the most he could make and still be below the 300 percent poverty level?

    a. $20,000
    b. $35,000
    c. $45,000
    d. $50,000

ObamaCare seeks to make health care more affordable by requiring every insurance plan to include many services, regarded as "essential health benefits." This requirement, however, applies only to plans put into effect after January 2014.

13. Which of the following is not one of these "essential health benefits"?

    a. Emergency services
    b. Over-the-counter medication
    c. Prescription medication
    d. Preventive care

14. Which of the following would be covered under "essential health benefits"?

    a. Hearing screening for adults
    b. Vision care for adults
    c. Vision care for children
    d. Dental care for adults

15. ObamaCare seeks to assist lower-income people who cannot afford health insurance. One of the ways it aims to accomplish this is by reducing deductibles. An insurance company might typically charge $500 for a medical service. The cost may be more; however, since you are covered by health insurance, your insurance company pays the rest. Sally, age fifty-six, slipped in her kitchen and needed hip surgery. She has a deductible of $500. After X-rays and surgical procedures, her total expense came to $15,000. Which of the following would apply?

    a. Sally would be forced to pay the entire $15,000.
    b. Sally would most likely pay a fee of $500 for the surgery.
    c. Sally would not have to pay anything.
    d. Sally would have to pay half the cost.

16. Haley is a fun-loving twenty-three-year-old who lives in Florida and enjoys going to the beach at least once a week. She will often lie in the sun for two hours to work on her tan and to lighten her strawberry blond hair. She usually remembers to wear sunscreen, but after reading an article about skin cancer, she doubts the effectiveness of this medication. She is glad that she recently enrolled in one of the marketplace health insurance plans and quickly schedules an appointment with her primary care physician. Which of the following would apply?

    a. As a preventive care service, her physician could offer her free counseling to educate her on ways to reduce her risk for skin cancer.
    b. As a preventive care service, her physician could combine the free counseling with a free skin cancer screening to assess any damage that may have been done.
    c. The skin cancer screening would be provided as a free preventive care service only if she has a gold- or platinum-level plan.
    d. The skin cancer counseling would be considered a covered service only if she has met her yearly deductible.

17. The physician tells Haley that she is perfectly healthy but that she should use a more effective sunscreen against prolonged exposure to sunlight. He prescribes a sunscreen that usually costs $50 without insurance. If her insurance company typically pays 70 percent of the prescription cost, which of the following represents the co-pay due at the pharmacy?

   a. $15
   b. $35
   c. $25
   d. There will be no co-pay

18. Bailey, thirteen, was found in her room unconscious. Kristen, her mother, discovered the painkillers she herself had been prescribed lying next to Bailey and called an ambulance. After detoxification, Bailey was sent to a facility for substance abuse therapy. Which of the following would apply?

   a. The therapy would be included under substance abuse treatment.
   b. The therapy would be in excess of the "essential health benefits," and she would be forced to pay out of pocket.
   c. The situation depends on her plan.
   d. None of the above

Questions 19 and 20 refer to the following scenarios.

   I.   Test strips for a young boy diagnosed with type-one diabetes
   II. A therapy session for a teenage boy experiencing mental trauma
   III. Cosmetic breast surgery for a healthy young woman
   IV. Cleft-palate surgery for a young girl

19. Which of the scenarios would result in the parent paying for the entire service(s)?

    a. II and III
    b. III only
    c. III and IV
    d. None of the above

20. Which of the scenarios would be considered outpatient care?

    a. II only
    b. I, II, and III
    c. IV only
    d. None of the above

Answers

1. C. Under ObamaCare, a child may stay on his or her parents' plan until age twenty-six. Choices A and B are incorrect because children do not have to get their own plan at age eighteen or twenty-one but can remain on their parents' plan. Choice D is irrelevant because enrolling in college does not affect children's health insurance, although a college may offer an alternative plan.

2. D. ObamaCare strives for universal health coverage. One way of making sure that happens is through the mandate stipulating that people without health insurance will be assessed a penalty that doesn't exceed the price of the insurance and will have to pay all of their health care expenses out of pocket. Therefore choice D is correct. Choice A is incorrect because a person will not be fined monthly. Choice B is incorrect because a person will not be ordered by a court to purchase insurance. Choice C is incorrect because a person will not be considered for Medicaid unless he or she applies for coverage and qualifies.

3. D. Under ObamaCare, health insurance providers may not charge higher premiums for people with pre-existing conditions, nor may they reject such applicants. Choice D is correct. Choices A and B are incorrect because charging a higher premium or rejecting an applicant based on a pre-existing condition is no longer permissible. "Essential health benefits" must also be covered by law. Choice C is wrong because ObamaCare forbids buying an incomplete plan.

4. A. ObamaCare requires scenario I, universal health coverage. Scenario II is incorrect because children can stay on their parents' plans until age twenty-six, not twenty-one. Scenarios III and IV are true because a health insurance company cannot deny coverage or charge more due to pre-existing conditions. Since scenarios I, III, and

IV are correct, the right choice is A, the only one that includes all the correct scenarios.

5. A. ObamaCare is the popular name for the Patient Protection and Affordable Care Act. Choice A is correct. Choices B, C, and D are incorrect.

6. B. Essential health benefits cover mental health problems. Stress is considered a mental health concern and therefore is covered by insurance plans. Choice A is reasonable because health facility staff will have to verify that the patient has health insurance. Choice C is also reasonable because if there is a problem calling for medication, the doctor can prescribe it. Answer D is rational because if a problem is better managed by someone who specializes in psychiatry, the doctor could refer the patient to a psychiatrist. Choice B, however, is not likely because mental health issues such as stress are legitimate health concerns covered by the essential benefits.

7. D. The correct answer is "All of the above." A unique feature of ObamaCare is a specialized marketplace known as the Small Business Health Options Program, or SHOP, for small businesses' health insurance transactions. SHOP helps businesses provide health coverage to their employees. As of 2014, until December 2015, only businesses with fewer than fifty full-time equivalent employees are eligible. It is anticipated that the threshold will be raised to a hundred such employees by January 1, 2016. Hence choice A is correct. Answer B is also correct because if a small business qualifies for SHOP, the owner and his or her spouse can also sign up for the program. Currently, ObamaCare considers a small business as one with fifty or fewer full-time employees, making choice C correct as well. Thus answer D, which encompasses all the correct choices, is the most appropriate.

8. D. Scenarios I and III are direct goals of ObamaCare. Scenario II might be an outcome of the fines and taxes, but it is not a direct goal. Scenario IV is irrelevant because not only is it not a direct goal of ObamaCare, but it is not a government initiative. This leaves only scenarios I and III. However, none of the choices specifies only I and III as the main goals of ObamaCare. That makes answer D correct, the only choice that encompasses these two scenarios.

9. A. The key to this question is to select not only the correct answer but the complete answer. It does not matter where your health insurance comes from as long as you are covered. You can have coverage from a private, state, or federally assisted provider. Choices C and D are incomplete because they mention only one option. Answer B mentions just two, making it incomplete as well. This leaves A as the complete and correct answer.

10. B. There were forty-five million to fifty million people without insurance as of July 2013. Choice A is incorrect because the figure is too low. Answers C and D are incorrect because the figures are too high. Choice B is correct because forty-four million is closest to the true range.

11. C. This is a chart-based question. Sara is part of a family of five: two parents and three children. Since her husband does not work, the total household income is $70,000. These are the two pieces of information needed to answer the question. Since $70,000 is roughly halfway between the 200 percent poverty cutoff (for a family of five, $55,000) and the 300 percent cutoff of $82,000, the best answer is a cutoff point in between. This is roughly equivalent to 250 percent of the poverty level, or answer C. Answer A is too low because Sara makes more than $41,355. Choice B is also too low since she makes more than $55,140. Answer is D incorrect because she makes less than $82,710.

ObamaCare Simplified

12. C. This is another chart- and math-based question. If the 300 percent threshold for poverty for a family of five is $82,000 and Peter's wife makes $35,000, he must make no more than $47,000 to qualify. Choices A and B are incorrect because if Peter makes that much, he will make less than the 300 percent threshold but will not maximize his income. Choice D is incorrect because if he makes that much money, he will surpass the 300 percent threshold. Answer C, $45,000, is the maximum he could make and still be below the 300 percent level.

13. B. The Affordable Care Act ensures that health plans offered in the individual and small-group markets, both inside and outside of the health insurance marketplace, offer a comprehensive package of items and services known as essential health benefits. These benefits must include items and services within at least the following ten categories: ambulatory patient services; emergency services; hospitalization; maternity and newborn care; mental health and substance use disorder services, including behavioral health treatment; prescription drugs; rehabilitative and habilitative services and devices; laboratory services; preventive and wellness services and chronic disease management, and pediatric services, including oral and vision care. Insurance policies must cover these benefits to be certified and offered in the health insurance marketplace. States expanding their Medicaid programs must provide these benefits to people newly eligible for Medicaid.

Choices A and D are incorrect because emergency and preventive care are covered under essential health benefits, and the question asks which of the following are not covered. Prescription medication is covered under essential health benefits, making C incorrect as well. This leaves B, over-the-counter medication, which is not covered by insurance.

14. C. Which services count under essential health benefits is still being debated; however, certain criteria have been established: Vision and dental services for children (but not for adults) are included under these benefits. Choices A, B, and D are incorrect because they specify hearing, vision, and dental services for adults. The best answer is C because it is well-established that children's vision care is covered under essential benefits.

15. B. Choice A is incorrect because Sally has insurance, so she does not have to pay for the entire surgery. Choice C is incorrect because most insurance plans do not cover the entire surgery. Similarly, answer D is incorrect because half the cost for the surgery would exceed the $500 deductible on her coverage.

16. A. Preventive care is covered in any ObamaCare plan, regardless of the level of the plan (i.e., bronze or silver). However, skin cancer screening is not considered a preventive care service; therefore, it would not be covered without patient cost sharing. Skin cancer behavioral counseling is a covered service because the United States Preventive Services Task Force recommends counseling individuals ten to twenty-four years old who have fair skin about minimizing their exposure to ultraviolet radiation to reduce risk for skin cancer. This means that the correct answer is A. The physician can offer skin cancer behavioral counseling without co-pay or co-insurance, regardless of whether the yearly deductible has been met.

17. A. There will be a co-pay because the insurance covers 70 percent of the cost. This makes answer D incorrect. If the insurance covers 70 percent, that means Haley has to pay 30 percent; and 30 percent of $50 is $15. Choice B is 70 percent of the cost of the sunscreen, and C is 50 percent of the cost. Since the company covers 70 percent, these numbers are too high.

18. A. Mental health is included under essential health benefits, which every plan must cover. If Bailey wished to enroll in a more intricate therapy, however, the insurance might not cover that. Choice B is incorrect because it says that substance abuse therapy is not covered, when it is. Answer C is incorrect because every plan is obliged to cover substance abuse treatment, including this one. Choice A is correct because substance abuse treatment is covered under any health insurance plan. Choice D, "None of the above," is incorrect.

19. B. Scenario I involves test strips for a young boy with type-one diabetes. Test strips can be covered under preventive care or chronic disease management. Scenario II is covered under mental health. The surgery in scenario IV is a matter of life or death because many children with this problem cannot swallow food properly. Scenario III is the only one not included under essential benefits. A parent would have to pay for all of the child's services only if the procedure is not covered under essential health benefits, which would be scenario III. The only choice that contains only scenario III is choice B.

20. Outpatient care consists of medical services administered to people who are not staying in a hospital or clinic overnight. The surgeries in scenarios III and IV require hospital visits, but only scenario IV requires a hospital stay. Most cosmetic breast surgeries are performed within a few hours as outpatient procedures. Mental health therapy sessions also do not require hospital stays. Scenario I involves test strips used to determine blood sugar level with the help of a portable device, a procedure that requires no hospitalization or overnight stay. Only scenario IV, which requires surgery for a cleft palate, involves a hospital stay. The only choice that contains scenarios I, II, and III is B.

Sources

Questions 1, 2, 3, 4, 5: Dean Obeidallah, S. (2013). Explain Obamacare at last. CNN. Retrieved 15 August 2013, from http://www.cnn.com/2013/07/29/opinion/obeidallah-explain-obamacare/

Question 7: Hoff, J. (2013). ObamaCare: Chief Justice Robert's Political Dodge. The Independent Institute. Retrieved 15 August 2013, from http://www.independent.org/pdf/tir/tir_18_01_01_hoff.pdf

Questions 8, 9, 10: Obamacarefacts.com,. What is ObamaCare / What is Health Care Reform?. Retrieved 15 August 2013, from http://obamacarefacts.com/whatis-obamacare.php

Questions 11, 12: U.S. Department of Health & Human Services,. 2013 Povery Guidelines. Aspe.hhs.gov. Retrieved 27 August 2014, from http://aspe.hhs.gov/poverty/13poverty.cfm

Questions 13, 14: Obamacarefacts.com,. Benefits Of ObamaCare: Advantage of ObamaCare. Retrieved 16 August 2013, from http://obamacarefacts.com/benefitsofobamacare.php

Question 15, 16, 18, 19, 20: Community Catalyst & Georgetown University Policy Institute,. Essential Benefits Package. Health Insurance 101. Retrieved 16 August 2013, from http://101.communitycatalyst.org/aca_provisions/essential_benefit_package

Question 16: Uspreventiveservicestaskforce.org,. Behavioral Counseling: Skin Cancer. Retrieved 16 August 2013, from http://www.uspreventiveservicestaskforce.org/uspstf/uspsskco.htm

Question 17: Amadeo, K. (2013). Obamacare in a Nutshell: Here's How it Affects You. About. Retrieved 17 August 2013, from http://useconomy.about.com/od/criticalssues/a/Obamacare-Summary.htm

CHAPTER 2

ObamaCare Health Exchange Basics

Introduction to the chapter: This chapter offers a basic look at the health exchange and how it works, including accessing the health plans, types of plans, information about income-based subsidies, the penalty tax, and how one qualifies for Medicaid under ObamaCare.

Objective of the chapter: The chapter will provide a basic understanding of the types of plans offered (e.g., what a gold plan entails). The true-or-false format of many of the questions will help dispel widespread inaccuracies about the nature of the health exchange under ObamaCare. Using simple scenarios, the chapter will also show how the tax penalty is derived and how qualifications for Medicaid are determined on the health exchange market.

Questions 1 to 6 have true and false answers regarding the health exchange. The exchange is a state-specific online marketplace where individuals and families can look for health insurance, including subsidized coverage. Subsidized insurance is discounted because the government pays a portion of the cost. If a statement is partially false, consider it entirely false.

Hamisu Salihu, MD, PhD

1. If I do not have access to a computer but want to investigate the online marketplace, I can go to specific locations in person.

    a. True
    b. False, because it is an online marketplace and there is no in-person consultation
    c. False, but not because of the reason stated above

2. I need health insurance, but my friends told me that I cannot purchase it on the health exchange. They said that I could only learn about different policies.

    a. The statement is true.
    b. The statement is false because the government requires that insurance be purchased through the online marketplace.
    c. The statement is false, but not because of the reason stated above.

3. Even if you are in prison, you can participate in the health exchange.

    a. True
    b. False, because incarcerated individuals are excluded from the exchange
    c. False, but not because of the reason stated above

4. I heard that only two kinds of health plans can be purchased on the health exchange market.

    a. True
    b. False

5. The gold plan is the most expensive and covers about 90 percent of medical fees.

   a. True
   b. False, because the most expensive plan is platinum
   c. False, because it is the least expensive

6. The excise tax is applied to a high-cost premium (Cadillac) plan; however, if this plan is purchased on the online marketplace, it is exempt from the tax.

   a. True
   b. False

7. If your annual salary is less than $15,000, you may qualify for Medicaid. What happens to those who have assets in addition? Do they qualify as well?

   a. Yes
   b. No, because assets are not technically considered income
   c. Maybe; it depends on the state
   d. Maybe; it depends on the type of asset and on the state

8. Health insurance is considered affordable if it does not consume more than a certain percentage of one's annual income. Which of the following is correct regarding affordable health insurance as a percentage of annual income?

   a. 20 percent of income
   b. 10 percent of income
   c. 8 percent of income
   d. 15 percent of income

9. If June makes $600,000 a year, what is the maximum amount that she can pay for health insurance for it to be considered affordable?

   a. $13,000
   b. $37,000
   c. $48,000
   d. $51,000

If you choose not to purchase health insurance, a penalty tax will be required. The tax, as shown below, will rise with the inflation rate. The amount you'll pay is either a fixed minimum or a percentage of your income, whichever is higher. The penalty tax applies to everyone except those belonging to at least one of the categories of exempted persons (e.g., members of certain religious groups and Native American tribes; undocumented immigrants, who are not eligible for health insurance subsidies under the law; incarcerated individuals; people whose incomes are so low they don't have to file taxes (currently $9,500 for individuals and $19,000 for married couples); people for whom health insurance is considered unaffordable (whose insurance premiums after employer contributions and federal subsidies exceed 8 percent of family income); and those going without insurance for less than three months in a row. The total penalty cannot exceed the national average of the annual premiums for a "bronze level" health insurance plan on ObamaCare exchanges for that year. The fee is applied for every month you go without insurance. You can go without minimum essential coverage for up to three months in a year. The penalty amounts to be paid for the coming years are shown below.

   2014: $95 per person per year or 1 percent of your income above the tax filing threshold
   2015: $325 per person per year or 2 percent of your income above the tax filing threshold
   2016: $695 per person per year or 2.5 percent of your income above the tax filing threshold

After 2016: $695 per person per year plus inflation adjustment or 2.5 percent of your income above the tax filing threshold

Note that for children (individuals under eighteen), the fixed penalty is halved (i.e., for 2014, $47.50; 2015, $162.50, and 2016, $347.50).

Use this information to answer questions 10 to 13.

10. Bo makes $1 million above the tax filing threshold every two years under his contract with a steel company. How much will he be expected to pay in 2016 if he does not have health insurance?

    a. $695
    b. $5,000
    c. $10,000
    d. d. $12,500

11. Paulo makes $600 a month working as a car salesman but refuses to pay for a health insurance policy. How much would he have to pay for an exemption tax in 2015?

    a. $144
    b. $325
    c. $600
    d. $0

12. Shay is a mother of two girls ages ten and twelve. She refuses to buy health insurance by 2016. If she makes $30,000 a year beyond the tax filing threshold, what would she pay as a penalty tax?

    a. $695
    b. $750
    c. $820
    d. $1,390

13. Ram has a wife and two minor children and plans on having health insurance, but it is April 2014. How much will he have to pay as a penalty? He makes $90,000 a year beyond the tax filing threshold, and his wife stays at home.

    a. $95
    b. $325
    c. $285
    d. $900

14. Brenda is incarcerated and wonders how her situation would affect her ability to receive health insurance. Which of the following scenarios would most likely apply?

    a. She would not be allowed to purchase insurance because prisoners are forbidden to have it.
    b. She would be allowed to review her options and pick from a variety of health insurance plans for prisoners.
    c. She would be given the same basic health plan as all the other inmates in the prison, a plan selected by the prison director.
    d. She would not be allowed to purchase or have any health plan, and her family would have to pay out of pocket for any emergency procedures.

15. Lupe is a mother of seven and works up to fourteen hours a day, but she has not been able to afford health insurance. She feels that her health is fading and wants to explore insurance options before she ends up in debt due to medical bills. The problem is that she is an illegal immigrant. Which of the following scenarios, if any, would apply?

    a. She would have no problem finding an insurance policy that provides coverage for her and her children.

b. She is not allowed to have coverage through the state health insurance exchanges. However, community clinics may offer help.
c. The federal government is obligated to cover her basic health care needs.
d. None of the above would be possible, because illegal immigrants are not allowed to receive any health services.

Questions 15 to 18 concern Medicaid. The following paragraph was taken from Medicaid.gov and explains what Medicaid is. The program usually covers individuals at 133 percent of the poverty level or lower but has been expanded in some states to 139 percent of the poverty mark. The chart below may also help in answering the questions.

"Medicaid and CHIP [Children's Health Insurance Program] provide health coverage to nearly 60 million Americans, including children, pregnant women, parents, seniors and individuals with disabilities. In order to participate in Medicaid, federal law requires states to cover certain population groups (mandatory eligibility groups) and allows the states the flexibility to cover other population groups (optional eligibility groups). States set individual eligibility criteria within federal minimum standards. States can apply to CMS [the Centers for Medicare and Medicaid Services] for a waiver of federal law to expand health coverage beyond these groups."

Household Size	100%	133%
1	$11,490	$15,282
2	15,510	20,628
3	19,530	25,975
4	23,550	31,322

16. Rikard thinks he may qualify for Medicaid. Which of the following scenarios would most likely not allow him to be eligible?

    a. He left his spouse while she was pregnant and refused to pay child support.
    b. He was incarcerated in the past.
    c. He has a stable job.
    d. He is reaping benefits from stock investments which, combined with his salary, push him to 150 percent of the poverty line.

17. Nisa was orphaned as a young girl and grew up in a foster home. At eighteen, she began an apprenticeship with an electrician. As she approaches the end of her education, she makes around $30 per service and performs roughly sixteen services per week. In a given year she makes around $25,000. She is twenty-four, has one daughter, and is pregnant with a son. Which of the following would most likely apply to her situation?

    a. She would most likely receive Medicaid benefits because she is pregnant.
    b. She would receive Medicaid benefits because she has a child.
    c. She would receive no Medicaid benefits because she is above the poverty mark and has a steady income.
    d. She might not receive Medicaid benefits because the number of people who can get Medicaid is capped in any given year.

18. Sean has two homes and collects enough rent to sustain him, but that is his only source of income. Which of the following best describes his eligibility for Medicaid?

    a. To qualify for Medicaid, he must spend down all of his assets including his properties.
    b. If Sean has no other assets, he will immediately qualify for Medicaid.

c. If Sean has no other assets, he will still not qualify because he has property, and having more than one property automatically removes him from the "needy" category.
d. There is not enough information to determine whether Sean will be eligible for Medicaid.

Questions 20 and 21 concern ObamaCare for small businesses.

19. Boris and Sheila Berg own ten antique stores and have approximately fifty-five employees. Which of the following situations is most likely what the Bergs will experience by 2016?

   a. If they are not providing their employees with health insurance, they will be required to cover at least 50 percent of them by 2016. If they do not, they will be required to pay a penalty.
   b. If they are offering their employees health insurance, they will be required to stop insuring them because only large businesses are allowed to offer health insurance.
   c. If they are not providing their employees with health insurance, they may be required to provide it for all of them. If they do not, they may face a penalty.
   d. Even if they are not offering their employees health insurance, they will not have to do so, because small businesses are exempt from the requirement.

20. If Jignesh owns several convenience stores with a total of forty-three employees and is offering his workers excessive or high-cost plans, which of the following may apply in 2018?

   a. A penalty that is 15 percent of the premium he pays per person
   b. An excise tax that is 40 percent of the premium he pays per person

c. None of the above because he will not be allowed to purchase high-cost or "Cadillac" plans without having legitimate reasons that require government approval
d. None of the above because he has fewer than a hundred employees and is therefore exempt from any taxes or penalties regarding high-cost plans

Answers

1. A. Choice A is correct because the marketplace can be accessed via mobile device or at specific locations in person. The government is intent on informing people about health insurance options and is using various approaches to do this.

2. C. The market is not only a place where people can learn about health insurance policies and decide which one is best; it is also a place where they can buy coverage. Hence choice A is incorrect. Answer B is incorrect because the government cannot require you to buy health insurance through the online marketplace. You may purchase a policy outside of the government health exchange market. Therefore the correct answer is C.

3. B. As the ObamaCare Health Exchange Handbook notes, there are valid exemptions from the requirement to purchase a health plan. These include illegal immigrant status, incarceration, and exemption from paying taxes. Those in jail fall under the category of incarceration and therefore cannot buy plans on the health exchange. This makes choice A incorrect. Answer B is correct because incarcerated people are excluded from the requirement. This makes choice C incorrect.

4. B. The correct answer to this question is "false." That is because there are four (and not two) choices or plans: bronze, silver, gold, and platinum. Answer A is therefore incorrect.

5. B. The correct answer to this question is "false." There are four plans: bronze, silver, gold, and platinum, ranked from least coverage to most. Bronze provides 60 percent coverage; silver offers 70 percent; gold provides 80 percent, and platinum offers 90 percent. This makes choice A incorrect. Answer C is wrong because the gold plan is not the least expensive; the bronze plan is.

6. B. The correct answer is "false." Answer A is incorrect. The high-cost premium plans are taxed regardless of who sells them to you. They are taxed at 40 percent of the total costs as explained in detail below. The online marketplace is a medium through which people can buy, companies can sell, and the government can subsidize health insurance. It does not offer exemptions from penalties or taxes. This makes choice A incorrect, because it mistakenly assumes that the online market can bypass taxes on premium plans.

   A premium or "Cadillac" plan is a health plan costing more than $10,200 for an individual or $27,500 for a family yearly, including worker and employer contributions to flexible spending or health savings accounts. The cost, however, excludes stand-alone vision or dental benefits. The tax will not take effect until 2018, giving health plans more time to benefit from possible cost savings from other reform measures. Employers with a high-risk pool will receive a break in the form of adjustment of the thresholds.

7. D. The key to this question is choosing the best answer. Answer A may be correct and is the most likely situation when considering what is counted toward Medicaid. Concerning eligibility, typically those with fewer assets and less income are more likely to qualify for Medicaid. Answer B mentions that states do not count assets in determining how much a person makes per year, which is false. Answer C is vague. Answer D is more comprehensive and is the preferred choice because it allows for variability. State policies vary appreciably, and so do people's situations. It is important to keep in mind that income is not calculated on salary alone but could include other sources of cash flow such as assets.

8. C. Answer C is correct because 8 percent of your annual income is the maximum that you are expected to pay toward health insurance. Choice A, 20 percent, is too high a number; a fifth of your income is considered too much for health coverage. Answer B, 10 percent, and

answer D, 15 percent, are also too high. The goal of requiring health insurance is not to drain people of their income but to ensure that they are sufficiently covered at an affordable rate for their own health and to avoid excessive emergency spending.

9. C. June makes $600,000 a year, and she can contribute a maximum of 8 percent of her income toward health coverage. The arithmetic needed to solve this problem is as follows: 0.08 × 600,000 = $48,000. Hence $48,000 is the maximum affordable contribution. Answer A, $13,000, and choice B, $37,000, are two low. Answer D is too high at $51,000. This leaves C as the correct choice.

10. D. If Bo makes $1 million every two years, he makes $500,000 per year. If he does not have health insurance in 2016, he will have to pay $695 per person per year or 2.5 percent of his income, whichever is greater. He could pay $695. To calculate 2.5 percent of his income, we multiply $500,000 by 0.025, the penalty rate for 2016. This comes out to $12,500. Since $12,500 is greater than $695, he is obligated to pay the higher amount. Answer A is incorrect because it does not take into account the fact that there are two possible ways the government will calculate the penalty. Since Bo makes more money than the average person, his penalty is higher than $695. Answer B is set for the wrong year, but if the same question were applied to the year 2014, this answer would be correct.

Similarly, if the same question were considered for 2015, then answer C would be correct; however, the year in this question is 2016. This leaves choice D as the only correct answer.

11. D. Paulo will pay no exemption tax. He makes $600 per month, and $600 × 12 = $7,200 per year. This amount is less than the tax filing threshold for a single individual. As illustrated in the table below, three main factors determine whether you have to file a tax return:

age, filing status, and income. The threshold amount is adjusted annually to account for inflation.

Tax filing earnings thresholds for 2013 taxes		
Filing status	Younger than 65	65 or older
Single	$10,000	$11,500
Head of household	$12,850	$14,350
Married filing jointly	$20,000 (both spouses)	$21,200 (one spouse 65 or older) $22,400 (both spouses 65 or older)
Qualifying widow/widower with dependent child	$16,100	$17,300
Married filing separately	$3,900	$3,900

Accessed and adapted from IRS Publications at http://www.irs.gov/publications/p17/ch01.html

12. D. In 2016, if Shay makes $30,000 per year beyond the tax filing threshold and there are three people in the family (one adult and two children under eighteen), she will have to pay $695 per person per year or 2.5 percent of her income, whichever is greater. We will calculate the penalty tax rate for 2016 for the three family members, bearing in mind that those under eighteen pay only half the fixed amount. The math goes like this: $695 for Shay + $695 halved for each child = $1,390. We will calculate 2.5 percent of her yearly income as follows: 0.025 x $30,000 = $750. Since the greater of these amounts is the penalty, Shay owes $1,390. Answer A does not take into account that there is more than one person in the household and therefore is incorrect. Answer B is the lesser of the two options, and that makes it incorrect. Answer C is too low. This makes D the correct choice.

13. D. In 2014, if Ram makes $90,000 a year beyond the tax filing threshold and there are four people in his family (two adults and two minors), he will have to pay $95 per adult person per year (and half of $95 per minor child per year) or 1 percent of his income, whichever is

greater. The first option will cost him $95 x 2 (for the two adults) + 95 halved x 2 (for the two minors), which comes to $285. The second option will cost him 0.01 x $90,000, which equals $900. He must pay the greater amount as his penalty. Choice A is incorrect because it fails to take into account the other family members, and because it is the lower penalty of $95. Answer B uses the price per person in 2015 as opposed to the one applicable in 2014. It also fails to take into account the presence of multiple family members. Answer C is incorrect because the penalty is too low; the higher option should be used to determine the penalty. This leaves choice D as the correct answer.

14. C. Answer A is incorrect because all are technically entitled to have health insurance if they are legal residents, even if they are in prison. Answer B is incorrect because inmates do not get to choose their plans; those who run the prison and negotiate options with private and government-subsidized companies select the plans for inmates. Choice C is correct because inmates receive health insurance plans that are largely the same, selected by the appropriate prison authority. Answer D is incorrect because the inmate will be insured, sparing the family from having to pay bills out of pocket.

15. B. The only health services that by law must be covered for undocumented immigrants are emergency services. Answer A says that private and state companies can provide the same health insurance plans to illegal immigrants as they provide to lawful residents (Lupe's US children), which is incorrect. ObamaCare does not allow illegal immigrants to participate in health exchange markets. However, options available to them include community-based health clinics/programs and safety-net hospitals, making choice B correct. Illegal immigrants could also buy private health insurance plans outside of the health exchange markets. Answer C is wrong because the federal government is not obligated to provide health services or insurance for illegal immigrants. Choice D is incorrect

because some programs are available to illegal immigrants through community-based services. Choice B is correct because it does not claim that illegal immigrants are allowed the same health care as legal immigrants or citizens, but it also does not deny that illegal immigrants can receive health services.

16. D. Medicaid evaluates the applicant's financial status, and past social issues are not typically assessed. Answer A relates to a past social issue, and even though what Rikard did may seem wrong, it does not prevent him from receiving health coverage from Medicaid. Answer B has a similar defect, because even if he has been to prison in the past, he may still qualify for assistance with health coverage if he does not make enough money. Answer C is incorrect because a stable job may still not pay enough to sustain him. How much that job pays is unclear, and so this choice provides insufficient information. Answer D, however, specifies not only that Rikard may be earning sufficient income but that he is above the 139 percent poverty range that qualifies an individual for Medicaid. This makes answer D correct. Medicaid officially helps people who are below 133 percent of the poverty line; however, in some states, that line may be extended to 139 percent.

17. A. More than one answer may be correct, but pregnant women are more likely to qualify for Medicaid. Answer B is incorrect because having a child adds a member to the household, but even with this increase, Nisa is not below the poverty line because she makes $25,000, which is greater than $20,000. Answer C is incorrect because Nisa might receive Medicaid benefits for being pregnant and bordering on the poverty line. This possibility makes C incorrect because it states categorically that she would not receive benefits. Answer D is incorrect because Medicaid is offered to those who are eligible; there is no cap on the number of people who can receive it. The correct choice is A, because women tend to receive more

benefits throughout pregnancy than are typically available for non-pregnant women.

18. D. This question mentions only that a man collects rent as his sole income. There is no mention of his tax bracket. The properties he owns could be worth millions of dollars, or they could be of low value. Answer A speculates that his assets and properties are worth too much for him to receive Medicaid, but we do not know how much the assets are worth. The answer may be right, but there is no concrete evidence to support this assertion. Answer B suggests that his property is not worth as much and that he will definitely qualify. Again this is mere speculation. The answer may be right, but there is no evidence to support this statement. Choice C again suggests that his assets are worth too much for him to receive Medicaid. The may be true, but again there is no evidence. Choice D is correct because there is insufficient information about his income to determine whether he will qualify for Medicaid.

19. C. To answer this question, it is important to know the requirements for a small business under ObamaCare. The law stipulates that by 2016, businesses of fifty employees or more must provide insurance that meets regulations or pay an "employer shared responsibility" penalty. Choice A is incorrect because employers must offer insurance to more than 50 percent of their employees; indeed, they may have to offer it to all employees. Answer B is incorrect because small businesses will not be required to stop offering health insurance to their employees. Choice D is incorrect because small businesses are required to provide health insurance. C is the correct answer because it states that a small business must offer insurance to all of its employees.

20. B. Choice B is correct because the excise tax applied to larger businesses is also applied to small businesses (those with fewer than fifty full-time employees). Answer A is incorrect because the

penalty is applied to those who do not have insurance, not to those with premium plans. In addition, this answer incorrectly refers to the amount owed as a 15 percent penalty.

Answer C is incorrect because private companies sell different plans, and it is possible to purchase premium plans. This choice wrongly states that it is not possible to purchase high-cost or "Cadillac" plans. Answer D is incorrect because small businesses are subject to most of the rules governing large businesses with a few possible exemptions. This leaves the answer choice B because in 2018 employers will be required to pay a 40 percent tax on any dollar amount beyond what is considered excess. There are always exceptions for which an exemption may be requested; however, the default policy is a 40 percent excise tax on excessive or "Cadillac" plans.

Sources

Questions 1, 2, 3, 4, 5, 6, 8: Obamacarefacts.com,. (2014). Health Insurance Exchange Guide. Retrieved 19 August 2013, from http://obamacarefacts.com/insurance-exchange/health-insurance-exchange-guide.php

Question 7: Caring.com,. Medicaid Eligibility. Retrieved 19 August 2013, from http://www.caring.com/ask/medicaid-eligibility-questions

Questions 9, 10, 11, 12: Obamacarefacts.com,. ObamaCare Individual Mandate. Retrieved 19 August 2013, from http://obamacarefacts.com/obamacare-tax-penalty.php

Question 11: Bankrate.com,. Who Has To File Taxes? | Bankrate.com. Retrieved 19 August 2013, from http://www.bankrate.com/finance/taxes/who-has-to-file-taxes-1.aspx

Question 13: National Association of Counties,. (2012). "County Jails and the Affordable Care Act: Enrolling Eligible Individuals in Health Coverage. Retrieved 5 September 2014, from http://www.naco.org/programs/csd/Documents/Health%20Reform%20Implementation/County-Jails-HealthCare_WebVersion.pdf

Question 14: Nilc.org,. Affordable Care Act - National Immigration Law Center. Retrieved 5 September 2014, from http://www.nilc.org/immigrantshcr.html

Question 17: Dubois Cary Law Group,. (2013). The Affordable Care Act: Finacial Security If You're Divorcing. Retrieved 5 September 2014, from http://www.duboislaw.net/blog/2013/06/the-affordable-care-act-financial-security-for-divorcing-women.shtml

Questions 15, 16, 18: Medicaid.gov,. Federal povery level charts. Retrieved 21 August 2013, from http://www.medicaid.gov/Medicaid-CHIP-Program-

Information/By-Topics/Eligibility/Downloads/2013-Federal-Poverty-level-charts.pdf

Questions 19, 20: Obamacarefacts.com,. ObamaCare Small Business Facts. Retrieved 21 August 2013, from http://obamacarefacts.com/obamacare-smallbusiness.php

CHAPTER 3

Pregnant Women, Illegal Immigrants, Medicaid and Medicare under ObamaCare

Introduction to the chapter: This chapter focuses on special/vulnerable populations that will be affected by the Affordable Care Act and the new health insurance regulations for these groups. This chapter will provide useful ideas (where to go, whom to contact, what to expect) to help these people obtain optimal affordable health coverage.

Objective of the chapter: This chapter will provide basic knowledge about what assistance exists to provide health coverage for vulnerable individuals including pregnant women and their infants, illegal immigrants, socio-economically disadvantaged populations, and the elderly.

Illegal immigrants are exempt from ObamaCare stipulations and are not required to obtain health insurance whether through the workplace or the health exchange. A draft bill known as the Immigration Bill of 2013, however, could grant eleven million undocumented immigrants provisional legal status. If enacted, the bill could accelerate the process through which illegal immigrants can attain permanent residency.

1. One consequence of not requiring illegal immigrants to have health insurance could be which of the following?

    a. More jobs given to illegal immigrants by large companies
    b. More jobs given to illegal immigrants by small companies
    c. Granting more jobs to individuals with provisional legal status
    d. All of the above

2. When can illegal immigrants receive health insurance through the marketplace?

    a. Anytime
    b. After they have been given provisional legal status
    c. After they have received citizenship
    d. Never

3. What was the status of the Immigration Bill of 2013 as of January 2014?

    a. Passed and enacted
    b. Reviewed and passed by the Senate only
    c. Reviewed and passed by the House of Representatives only
    d. Rejected

States have the option to extend Medicaid coverage to pregnant women living at up to 185 percent of the poverty line or beyond, and most states have done so. In addition, some states have programs that allow pregnant women with incomes above the medically needy threshold to be eligible if their health expenses are sufficiently high.

4. What is the highest level of income at which pregnant women can receive Medicaid benefits?

    a. Below 100 percent of the poverty line
    b. Below 133 percent of the poverty line
    c. Below 139 percent of the poverty line
    d. Below 185 percent of the poverty line

5. Which of the following services are included under extended Medicaid coverage for pregnant women?

    a. Labor
    b. Delivery
    c. Complications
    d. All of the above

6. Approximately what percentage of births in the United States does Medicaid finance?

    a. 5%
    b. 20%
    c. 40%
    d. 70%

The following paragraph concerns Medicaid eligibility when income changes after establishment of eligibility:

"Once eligibility is established, pregnant women remain eligible for Medicaid through the end of the calendar month in which the 60th day after the end of the pregnancy falls, regardless of any change in family income."

7. Laura is pregnant and has been found eligible for Medicaid benefits. If her husband, who was previously unemployed, found a job that pays $500,000 per year, which of the following would best describe what would happen to her Medicaid benefits?

   a. Laura would still be eligible for Medicaid benefits because once eligibility is established, Medicaid coverage will continue until the end of the pregnancy and sixty days after delivery.
   b. Laura would no longer be eligible for Medicaid benefits as of the end of the month in which her husband received his first paycheck.
   c. Medicaid would cover prenatal care, labor, and delivery; however, it would no longer cover postpartum care.
   d. None of the above

The following paragraph is specific to the program in California but is an example of Medicaid-based programs that reach out to low-income individuals:

"Starting in January 2014, Medi-Cal will have expanded to cover all low-income individuals, ages 19 to 64, who are U.S. citizens or national or legal permanent residents for at least 5 years, and are not pregnant. Those who are pregnant qualify for another type of insurance."

8. Which of the following statements is true?

   a. Low-income individuals are those whose taxable income is within 100 percent of the poverty level.
   b. Low-income individuals are those whose taxable income is within 150 percent of the poverty level.
   c. Low-income individuals are those whose taxable income is within 200 percent of the poverty level.
   d. None of the above

9. Does the Affordable Care Act address homeless people?

   a. Yes
   b. No
   c. In some cases, but not all

Before delving into health care for the homeless, it is important to understand what homelessness looks like. Questions 10 and 11 deal with this issue.

10. Which of the following choices reflects what homelessness looks like in the United States?

    a. Mostly African-American and Hispanic people
    b. Mostly unemployed, single, and drug abusers
    c. Veterans and unemployed disabled people
    d. A group diverse in ethnicity and situation

According to the Kaiser Family Foundation, "persons experiencing homelessness are disproportionately affected by high rates of both chronic disease and acute illness, and many of these conditions are associated with and exacerbated by their living situations. Mental health conditions, alcohol and substance abuse, and chronic disease (such as diabetes, hypertension, cardiovascular disease, and chronic obstructive pulmonary disease) are all prevalent among this population. Individuals experiencing homelessness also have high rates of HIV, tuberculosis, pneumonia, and asthma."

11. On any given night, about how many people are homeless in the United States?

    a. 6,000
    b. 60,000.
    c. 600,000.
    d. 6,000,000.

12. According to the Kaiser Family Foundation, many adults within the homeless population are not eligible for Medicaid. Which of the following changes were implemented by January 2014?

    a. Making the application process for health coverage for the homeless much easier
    b. Increasing coverage among low-income individuals to include homeless people
    c. Both a and b
    d. Neither a nor b

The following chart shows the health insurance status of groups of people in the United States (whether they are uninsured, covered by Medicaid, or another type of insurance). Questions 13, 14, and 15 are based on this chart.

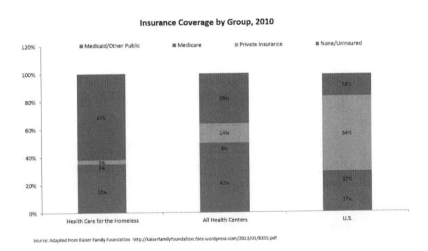

Source: Adapted from Kaiser Family Foundation http://kaiserfamilyfoundation.files.wordpress.com/2013/01/8355.pdf

13. According to the chart, which of the following is correct?

    a. Nearly 62 percent of homeless people are without health coverage.
    b. Nearly 30 percent of homeless people are without health coverage.

c. Seventeen percent of all people in the United States are without health insurance.
d. None of the above

14. According to the chart, which of the following is incorrect?

    a. Thirty-eight percent of homeless people are insured.
    b. Fifty percent of people in all health centers have Medicaid or Medicare.
    c. Roughly half of the US population is covered through private insurance companies.
    d. None of the above, because a, b, and c are all correct

15. According to the chart, which of the following is correct?

    a. The information presented in the chart is based on past surveys and is no longer valid.
    b. The information presented in the chart is relevant up to July 2013.
    c. The information presented in the chart is not based on current data; however, the chart presents reasonable information that can be used to assess trends.
    d. The date for the information presented in the chart is irrelevant to understanding trends.

16. Which approach best describes the way the poor and the homeless will be informed about health care options for them?

    a. Large groups will convene in inner cities to discuss options.
    b. Small advising groups will target specific people to discuss options.
    c. The media will cover options and expect the word to spread.
    d. The homeless will have to take the initiative and seek out the information for themselves.

Questions 17 to 20 concern Medicare. The following paragraph briefly defines the program.

"Medicare is the federal health insurance program for people who are 65 or older, certain younger people with disabilities, and people with End-Stage Renal Disease (permanent kidney failure requiring dialysis or a transplant, sometimes called ESRD)."

17. What is the primary difference between Medicaid and Medicare?

    a. Medicaid is generally for younger, healthier people, while Medicare is typically for older persons.
    b. Medicaid is for the poor, while Medicare is for the average person.
    c. Medicaid is for older persons, while Medicare is typically for younger adults and children.
    d. Medicaid is for the homeless, while Medicare is for the needy who have a home.

Questions 18, 19, and 20 are based on the following information:

There are four kinds of Medicare plans: Health Maintenance Organizations (HMOs), Preferred Provider Organizations (PPOs), Private Fee-for-Service Plans, and Special Needs Plans.

18. Which plans best fit the following description? Networks of health care providers are available to participants. These plans are usually cost-effective alternatives to normal health care plans.

    a. HMOs
    b. PPOs
    c. Private Fee-for-Service Plans
    d. Special Needs Plans

19. Which type of plan is best described by the following feature? The plan determines how much it will pay doctors, other health care providers, and hospitals, and how much you must pay when you get care.

    a. HMOs
    b. PPOs
    c. Private Fee-for-Service Plans
    d. Special Needs Plans

20. Which plans are best described by the following features? They "limit membership to people with specific diseases or characteristics, and tailor their benefits, provider choices, and drug formularies (list of covered drugs) to best meet the specific needs of the groups they serve."

    a. HMOs
    b. PPOs
    c. Private Fee-for-Service Plans
    d. Special Needs Plans

Answers

1. D. Under ObamaCare, small and large employers may hire more illegal immigrants, file for exemption, and avoid a penalty since the companies are not required to provide health insurance for them. This could save the companies money. Hence the responses in A and B are correct. The same reasoning could be applied to the case of immigrants with provisional legal status. This status is part of the 2013 Immigration Bill, which has been approved by the Senate but is still being reviewed by the House. Under the bill, persons enjoying provisional legal status would be barred from receiving government benefits and would have to pay back taxes. They would not be required to have health insurance, making them attractive for employment by companies. Answers A, B, and C are true, so the correct response is choice D.

2. C. The correct answer is that illegal immigrants will be able to receive health insurance through the marketplace after they have become citizens. Answer A is incorrect because the law specifically states that illegal immigrants cannot receive health insurance through the marketplace under ObamaCare. Choice B is incorrect because illegal aliens must become to receive health insurance. Provisional legal status is only the first step to becoming a citizen. Answer D is incorrect because once illegal immigrants become citizens they have the rights of all other naturalized citizens regardless of their previous status, including health insurance privileges under ObamaCare.

3. B. The correct answer is that this bill had been reviewed and passed only by the Senate as of January 2014. The House of Representatives will review the bill and decide its fate. Answer A is incorrect because the bill had not been enacted as of January 2014. Choice C is incorrect because the House has not passed the bill. Answer D is not correct because the process of examining the bill is not yet complete, and so the bill has not been rejected. Choice B is correct because the bill

was approved in the Senate and then moved to the House where it awaits action.

4. D. The answer to this question is 185 percent of the poverty line, the figure stated in the paragraph above the question. The percentage applies only to pregnant women. Answer A is incorrect because it is the poverty mark and doesn't apply specifically to pregnancy. Answer B is incorrect because Medicaid usually covers 133 percent of the poverty mark for basic health coverage for all persons, including pregnant and nonpregnant women. Answer C is incorrect because Medicaid is extended in many states to cover those up to 139 percent of the poverty line. This level, however, is still below the highest level of income for eligibility allowed for pregnant women. Choice D correctly states 185 percent of the poverty level. Note that the paragraph above the questions said that coverage depends on the state but that most states cover those up to or over 185 percent of the poverty mark.

5. D. The answer is "all of the above" because coverage for pregnancy includes "Medicaid coverage for prenatal care through pregnancy, labor, and delivery, and for 60 days postpartum as well as other pregnancy-related care." Answer A is correct and so are choices B and C.

6. C. Medicaid reports that it finances 40 percent of all births in the United States. This makes Medicaid a key player in healthy childbirth and maternal health. Answer A is incorrect because it is too low; it is about one tenth of the correct percentage. Answer B is also too low because 20 percent is half of 40 percent. Choice D is too high.

7. A. The correct answer is that Medicaid will not change coverage after eligibility has been established. The usual coverage includes "prenatal care through the pregnancy, labor, and delivery, and for 60 days postpartum as well as other pregnancy-related care," and

this will continue to be the case. Answer B is incorrect because it says that Laura will no longer be eligible for benefits. Answer C is incorrect because it says that Medicaid will provide limited coverage in her situation. Once eligibility has been established, Medicaid will provide full coverage regardless of a change in family income. Since choice A is correct, answer D should be disregarded.

8. B. This is the correct answer because, according to the US Department of Education, the term "low-income individual" means a person whose family's taxable income for the preceding year did not exceed 150 percent of the poverty level amount. This makes choice A incorrect because 100 percent of the poverty level is too low a threshold. Answer C is incorrect because 200 percent is too high a threshold to be considered low-income. Choice D becomes unnecessary since the correct answer is one of the above.

9. A. The answer to this question is yes. Although few people know about the benefits offered by ObamaCare, insurance for the poor is included under the category of low-income individuals. The homeless will have more access to health care.

10. D. This is the correct answer because homelessness has a multitude of causes. Although there may be more homelessness in some ethnic groups as compared with others, the homeless population is mixed, as are the reasons for this predicament. According to the Kaiser Family Foundation, "Frontline staff reported working with individuals of all races, ethnicities, and immigration status and noted that their clients also vary in age, family status, and length of homelessness. They also described a range of backgrounds and personal experiences among the homeless population, including military veterans, domestic violence victims, and previously incarcerated individuals." Answer A is incorrect because a large percentage of Caucasians are also homeless; although there may be trends, homelessness is not limited to black and Hispanic communities. Answer B is also

incorrect because many homeless people are temporarily homeless, previously incarcerated, or veterans. Choice C is incorrect because it includes only two groups out of several that can be homeless. The correct answer is D, a diverse group from different backgrounds and different circumstances.

11. C. The correct answer is six hundred thousand people. According to a survey in January 2011, there were 636,017 homeless people in the United States. Answer A is too low and is about a hundred times less than the actual number of homeless. Answer B is incorrect because it is ten times smaller than the true number. Answer D is about ten times greater than the actual number. If there were 311 million people in the United States in 2011 when the number of homeless was gathered, and 636,000 were found to be homeless, the percentage of homeless would be 0.2. Sources differ on the figure, but it ranges from 0.2 percent to 0.5 percent. Note that the number of homeless people on a given night, as opposed to the population of homeless individuals, is calculated differently.

12. C. Both A and B are correct because not only will the process become more streamlined but the coverage will increase to include most individuals. Answer A is correct because as of now, many homeless people have difficulty reading, understanding, or even finding the means to fill out applications, especially when many of these people do not have stable contact information. Revisions to the application process should make it easier to apply for such aid. Furthermore, a larger number of people will be covered under Medicaid due to an extension of the program. Previously, many homeless individuals were not covered, but this will no longer be the case. Since both A and B are correct, the right answer is C.

13. A. This is the correct choice because 62 percent of homeless people are without coverage. The bar "Health Care for the Homeless" is the one relevant to this question. The white space represents the 62

percent of homeless people who are uninsured. Answer B is incorrect because 30 percent of homeless people are insured under Medicaid, as designated by the dark blue space in the column marked "Health Care for the Homeless." Answer C is also incorrect because 17 percent of the people in the column marked "U.S." have Medicaid coverage, denoted by the dark blue shading. Since the correct answer is A, choice D is irrelevant.

14. D. This choice is correct because answers A, B, and C are correct. Answer A is correct because in the column marked "Health Care for the Homeless," any color shading denotes those who are insured. The addition of these percentages, 3, 5, and 30, equals 38 percent. Answer B is correct because in the column marked "All Health Centers," the colors blue and dark blue represent those with Medicaid (42 percent) or Medicare (8 percent), totaling 50 percent. Choice C is also correct because the column marked "U.S." shows that 54 percent of people have health insurance with private companies (light blue shading).

15. C. This is the correct choice because the information presented in the chart is from 2010 but was published in 2011. Answer A is incorrect because it says that the data are no longer useful. In fact, they provide a baseline perspective to compare with future insurance coverage trends. Answer B is incorrect because it fails to observe that the data are indeed from 2010 and therefore are not up to date. Choice D says that the date does not matter in helping to understand trends. Although two years is a relatively short time to use in describing trends, that does not completely negate the relevance of the information for future trend analysis. Answer C is correct because it acknowledges that the information is not up to date but explains that a reasonable trend can still be assessed using this information.

16. B. Studies have shown that many homeless people distrust public systems and government in general and therefore require a more personal approach to convince them of the benefits of systems such

as health insurance. A report from the Kaiser Family Foundation says that sometimes it is necessary to approach people where they live (e.g., under a bridge) and speak with them about how they may qualify for health insurance. This approach prevents them from being overwhelmed with information while providing a familiar environment that favors assimilation of information. Answer A does not include the personal approach that is the goal of the system and is therefore incorrect. The same applies to choice C. Not only do newspapers and other types of media require access to the Internet for free information, but they lack the personal touch needed. Answer D presumes that people who are not aware of benefits will seek out the information for themselves. This makes choice B the correct answer.

17. A. The correct answer is that Medicaid is for the younger and for the generally healthier, while Medicare is for the older; the paragraph above the question says that Medicare is for those sixty-five and up. Since the other choices do not mention that Medicare is for the elderly, they are wrong. Answer B is incorrect because the differentiating factor is not income. Answer C states the opposite of what is true. Answer D is wrong because Medicaid is for both the needy and the homeless, and this choice does not state the program's correct purpose. Medicare is "the federal health insurance program for people who are 65 or older, certain younger people with disabilities, and people with End-Stage Renal Disease." This implies that it is primarily for those older than sixty-five.

18. A. The answer is HMOs. The Texas Department of Insurance says, "Health maintenance organizations (HMOs) are managed care plans that provide health care to their members through contracted networks of doctors and hospitals. HMOs are popular alternatives to traditional health care plans because they usually cost less." According to the official US government site for Medicare, PPOs are "a type of Medicare Advantage Plan (Part C) offered by a private insurance

company. In a PPO Plan, you pay less if you use doctors, hospitals, and other health care providers that belong to the plan's network. You pay more if you use doctors, hospitals, and providers outside of the network." Since this plan is offered by a private insurance company and allows coverage outside of the network, it is a different type of plan and choice B is incorrect. Answer C is also incorrect because a distinctive characteristic of a Private Fee-for-Service Plan is that "the plan determines how much it will pay doctors, other health care providers, and hospitals, and how much you must pay when you get care," according to the US government site for Medicare. Since this definition does not match the description provided, this plan is not the answer. Finally, the Special Needs Plan is also incorrect because, according to the government site for Medicare, this plan "limit(s) membership to people with specific diseases or characteristics, and tailor(s) their benefits, provider choices, and drug formularies (list of covered drugs) to best meet the specific needs of the groups they serve." Because this differs from the description provided, the answer is incorrect.

19. C. The answer is a Private Fee-for-Service Plan. This is the only plan that matches the description provided in the question. Answer A is incorrect because an HMO offers "networks of healthcare providers that are available to people with these types of plans. They are usually cost-effective alternatives to normal healthcare plans." Answer B is also incorrect because a PPO operates similarly to an HMO but charges more for health care providers outside of the network. Since this differs from the description provided, it is also incorrect. Choice D is incorrect because Special Needs Plans are offered only to people who have certain special needs and are tailored specifically to them. Since the description in the question is more general, this answer is incorrect. Choice C is the only plan that matches the description perfectly.

20. D. Special Needs Plan is the correct answer because it is the only plan that selects people based on certain health characteristics. HMOs and PPOs are more general and accept anyone regardless of medical conditions, making these choices incorrect. Private Fee-for-Service Plans are organized based more on money than on special needs. Thus this is also an incorrect answer.

Sources

Question 1, 2, 3: Immigrationpolicy.org,. (2013). Special Reports | Immigration Policy Center. Retrieved 5 September 2014, from http://www.immigrationpolicy.org/special-reports/guide-s744-understanding-2013-senate-immigration-bill

Questions 1, 2, 3: Cox, R. (2013). Cruz: Immigration bill, ObamaCare create 'enormous incentive' to hire immigrants. TheHill. Retrieved 5 September 2014, from http://thehill.com/blogs/floor-action/senate/307761-cruz-immigration-bill-obamacare-create-enormous-incentive-to-hire-immigrants

Questions 4, 5, 6, 7: Medicaid.gov,. Pregnant Women | Medicaid.gov. Retrieved 5 September 2014, from http://www.medicaid.gov/Medicaid-CHIP-Program-Information/By-Population/Pregnant-Women/Pregnant-Women.html

Questions 8, 9, 10: The Huffington Post,. (2014). Passing Obamacare Seems Easy Compared To This. Retrieved 5 September 2014, from http://www.huffingtonpost.com/2013/06/02/homeless-affordable-care-act_n_3366148.html

Question 9: Www2.ed.gov,. (2014). Federal TRIO Programs Current-Year Low-Income Levels. Retrieved 5 September 2014, from http://www2.ed.gov/about/offices/list/ope/trio/incomelevels.html

Questions 10, 11, 12, 13, 14, 15, 16: Kaiser Family Foundation,. (2012). Retrieved 10 September 2013, from http://kaiserfamilyfoundation.files.wordpress.com/2013/01/8355.pdf

Question 11: U.S. Department of Housing and Urban Development,. (2010). Retrieved 10 September 2013, from http://www.huduser.org/publications/pdf/5thHomelessAssessmentReport.pdf

Questions 17, 18, 19, 20: Medicare.gov,. (2014). About Medicare health plans | Medicare.gov. Retrieved 5 September 2014, from http://www.medicare.gov/sign-up-change-plans/medicare-health-plans/medicare-health-plans.html

Questions 18, 19, 20: U.S. Department of Health and Human Services,. (2011). Retrieved 5 September 2014, from http://www.medicare.gov/Pubs/pdf/11302.pdf

CHAPTER 4

Dental and Eye Care under ObamaCare: Part 1

Introduction to the chapter: This is the first of two chapters on dental and eye care under ObamaCare and will address what is covered, who is covered, and resources for coverage for specific populations and conditions.

Objective of the chapter: After answering the questions in this chapter, readers will have a better understanding of eye and dental preventive care as part of the "essential health benefits" under ObamaCare; the beneficiaries of preventive eye and dental care; government subsidies for such care, and Medicare and Medicaid coverage for this care.

Read the scenarios and questions below carefully. Although consecutive questions may look the same, they are different.

1. Pat and her daughter walk into a clinic for eye examinations. They are covered by an insurance plan purchased through the health exchange. Which of the following scenarios is correct given that Pat is forty-six and her daughter is twelve?

    a. Both of them will be taken care of because all basic health plans cover vision for everyone.

b. Neither of them will be taken care of because vision is not covered by the basic health plan; vision insurance is separate.
c. Only the mother will be covered because vision is covered only under adult plans.
d. Only the daughter will be covered because vision is covered only for children with basic health plans.

2. Pat and her daughter walk into a clinic for dental examinations. Which of the following scenarios is correct given that Pat is forty-six and her daughter is twelve?

    a. Both of them will be taken care of because all basic health plans cover dental care for everyone.
    b. Neither of them will be taken care of because dental care is not covered by the basic health plan; the dental plan is separate.
    c. Only the mother will be covered because dental care is covered only under adult plans.
    d. Only the daughter will be covered because dental care is covered only for children with basic health plans.

3. John is twenty-two and still on his parents' plan. He broke a tooth. Will he be covered for fixing it?

    a. Yes. Since he is still under his parents' health insurance, he will be considered a child until age twenty-six.
    b. Yes. He is still under his parents' health insurance, and as long as he is under twenty-four, he will receive all the benefits of pediatric care.
    c. No. Since he is no longer considered a child, he no longer receives pediatric benefits.
    d. No. He can no longer be under his parents' plan because he is older than twenty-one.

4. If Paulina, ten, needs dental braces, will her mother's basic health plan be required to cover them starting in 2014?

   a. No, because orthodontia (treatment of teeth irregularities like misalignment) is not considered an essential health benefit unless it is medically necessary
   b. Yes, because orthodontia is considered medically necessary and is covered by all basic health plans
   c. Yes, because orthodontic care is expensive and should be affordable by everyone even if it is not medically necessary
   d. No, because orthodontic care is not considered medical care and therefore requires separate dental insurance

5. Although basic health plans are not required to include dental care for adults, supplementary plans can facilitate dental care.

   a. False, because basic health plans do cover dental health for adults; they just do not cover orthodontic care
   b. True, because although dental care is not among the essential benefits, concessions have been made to give people the option to purchase inexpensive dental coverage
   c. False, because dental plans are a completely separate entity that requires a separate plan
   d. None of the above

6. Approximately how many children are expected to benefit from the inclusion of pediatric dental coverage under ObamaCare?

   a. Thirty thousand
   b. Three hundred thousand
   c. Three million
   d. Thirty million

7. How many Americans live in areas without access to dental care?

   a. 30,000
   b. 300,000
   c. 3,000,000
   d. 30,000,000

8. Is proper dental care medically essential?

   a. Yes, because dental care can protect against diseases such as oral infections
   b. Yes, because dental care can prevent diseases such as diabetes
   c. Yes, because dental care can prevent health problems such as cardiovascular disease
   d. All of the above

9. Government subsidies will cover dental insurance for adults.

   a. True
   b. False
   c. Depends on the situation

10. Essential health benefits include pediatric dental care; however, on the health exchange, purchasing the dental component is not mandatory.

    a. True
    b. False
    c. Depends on the situation

11. The American Dental Association supports adult dental coverage for emergencies as part of the essential health benefits package. Which of the following describes the government reaction to this concern?

    a. No reaction
    b. Emergency coverage that pays 50 percent of the costs regardless of the plan
    c. Emergency coverage that pays 25 percent of the costs regardless of the plan
    d. Inclusion of emergency dental care as part of the essential health benefits

12. Dental insurance providers will be allowed to use age, tobacco use, and a person's place of residence and family composition to calculate premiums as well as coverage for dependents up to age twenty-six. Which of the following is an appropriate reaction to this statement?

    a. This statement is true because most insurers are private entities and are allowed to charge extra for pre-existing conditions and other predispositions.
    b. This statement is true because dental insurance is independent of the insurance covered by ObamaCare.
    c. This statement is false because insurance is now a public enterprise and companies are not allowed to charge higher premiums for pre-existing conditions and other predispositions.
    d. None of the above

13. Although basic health plans are not required to include vision care for adults, supplementary plans can facilitate this care.

    a. False, because basic health plans do cover vision health for adults
    b. True, because although vision care is not among the essential benefits, concessions have been made to give people the option of purchasing supplementary vision coverage

c. False, because vision plans are a completely separate entity that requires a separate plan
d. None of the above

14. Medicare and Medicaid cover routine adult eye exams for glasses or contacts. Which of the following is an accurate response to this statement?

    a. That's not true because adult vision care is not included under other basic health insurance plans.
    b. That is true because adult vision care is included under other health insurance.
    c. That is true because eyeglasses and contacts are considered essential medical treatments.
    d. None of the above

15. Government subsidies will cover vision care plans.

    a. True
    b. False
    c. Depends on the situation

According to the Centers for Disease Control and Prevention, "Vision loss is a serious public health problem in the United States and will get worse in the next 30 years because of the aging population, increase in chronic diseases affecting the eye and vision, and changing demographics of the U.S. population.

In 2000, more than 3.4 million Americans aged 40 years or older were visually impaired or blind, and this number is projected to reach 5.5 million by 2020."

16. By what percentage can cases be reduced through preventive eye care?

    a. 10%
    b. 30%
    c. 50%
    d. 70%

17. Which of the following is a valid description of ocular health in the United States?

    a. Ocular health is uniform across the fifty states.
    b. Ocular health is uniform across all racial groups.
    c. Ocular health is uniform across all age groups.
    d. Ocular health varies among states as well as among racial and age groups.

18. What is glaucoma?

    a. Near-sightedness
    b. Far-sightedness
    c. Tunnel vision
    d. Pressure buildup in the eye that can damage the optic nerve

19. Why is preventing glaucoma important?

    a. It is not important because glaucoma is not preventable.
    b. It is important because glaucoma is a common but preventable cause of vision loss.
    c. A separate vision insurance plan is required to cover glaucoma screening.
    d. Treatment is covered by any health insurance.

20. Medicaid covers glaucoma screenings for those who demonstrate high risk. Which of the following are considered high-risk factors?

    a. Family history
    b. Medical history
    c. Race
    d. All of the above

Answers

1. D. This is the correct answer because dental and vision care are covered only for children under the essential health benefits. Answer A is incorrect because dental care is not in the basic health plan for everyone since adults are not covered. Choice B is incorrect because Pat's daughter can receive dental and vision treatment under basic health benefits. Answer C is incorrect; the mother will not be covered since she is more than eighteen or twenty-one (depending on the state).

2. D. This answer is correct because dental and vision care are covered only for children under the essential health benefits. Answer A is incorrect because dental care is not in the basic health plan for everyone; adults are not covered. Choice B is incorrect because Pat's daughter can receive dental and vision treatment under basic health benefits. Answer C is incorrect; the mother will not be covered because she is more than eighteen or twenty-one (depending on the state).

3. C. This answer is correct because pediatric care covers patients until age eighteen or twenty-one, depending on the state. Only pediatric vision and dental care are covered by the essential health benefits; adults are excluded even if they are on their parents' plans. Answer A is incorrect because it says that adults can be on their parents' plan and receive pediatric benefits past age twenty-one. Choice B is incorrect because it implies that pediatric benefits continue until age twenty-four. The age limit is eighteen or twenty-one, depending on the state. The answer also implies that the age limit for remaining on a parent's health insurance plan is twenty-four, which is also not correct. The limit is twenty-six. Answer D is incorrect, again because John can remain on his parents' plan until he is twenty-six.

4. A. This choice is correct because actions deemed medically necessary are covered under the essential health benefits. This question is a prime example because braces are not considered medically necessary except in rare circumstances. Given their cosmetic purpose, they are not covered under pediatric dental care. This makes answer B incorrect because it assumes braces are generally medically necessary. Answer C is incorrect because it tries to justify insurance coverage for nonessential treatment simply by arguing that some people cannot afford it, which does not change what is considered medically essential under ObamaCare. Choice D is incorrect because orthodontic care is considered medical care; it is just not always essential.

5. B. This answer is correct because dental care is not covered for adults but is provided as an add-on option to basic plans. Answer A is incorrect because basic plans do not cover dental care for adults. Choice C is incorrect because dental plans need not be purchased from a different company altogether or even from a different plan. Since there are options that allow supplementary dental plans, answer D is also incorrect.

6. C. Answer C is right because three million children will benefit from the inclusion of pediatric dental care in the essential health benefits. Answers A and B are incorrect because they are significantly lower than the correct figure. Choice D is too high.

7. D. This is the correct answer because thirty-three million Americans live in places that do not have enough dentists or offer sufficient dental care to meet oral care needs. Answers A, B, and C are too low.

8. D. This answer is right because all of the other choices are correct. Answer A is correct because bacterial buildup in the mouth can cause oral infections. Answer B is correct because studies have shown that without proper dental care, patients are at a higher risk for developing

diabetes. Choice C is also correct because buildup of plaque in the mouth and buildup of plaque in the arteries are not too different. The plaque that builds up in the mouth breaks off and enters the blood system. Once in the bloodstream, it can recoagulate, increasing the risk of plaque accumulation within blood vessels. Treating dental plaque before it enters the bloodstream can reduce this risk, which means dental care can prevent cardiovascular disease.

9. B. The correct answer is "false" because dental insurance plans will not be made mandatory and therefore will not be subsidized (as of July 2013). Answer A is incorrect because it says that adults can receive dental insurance subsidies. Choice C is incorrect because for the most part dental coverage is not situational and is based on whether the patient is an adult or a child. If the patient is a child, preventive dental care is offered as part of the essential health benefits under ObamaCare.

10. A. The correct answer is "true." Answer B is incorrect because purchasing pediatric dental care is not mandatory, even as an essential health benefit, on the health exchange. The law requires that a pediatric dental plan be available, but you do not have to buy it. Choice C is incorrect because no situations need be considered; even adults with dependents are not required to purchase pediatric dental insurance.

11. A. There was no reaction because the government took no steps to include coverage for dental emergencies. As far as the law is concerned, patients without dental plans will be treated for dental emergencies but will have to pay 100 percent of treatment costs. Choice B is incorrect because there is no coverage, so the patient would have to pay 100 percent of costs, not 50 percent. Answer C is incorrect for the same reason; the patient would have to pay 100 percent of costs, not 75 percent. Answer D is incorrect because once

again there is no coverage. The government has not changed that, so emergency dental treatment is still not an essential health benefit.

12. B. This answer is correct because dental insurance is, in fact, independent of other health insurance. Because of this, it is not subject to the same regulation as medical health insurance under ObamaCare. Answer A is incorrect because health insurance is not entirely privatized. The crux of ObamaCare is government regulation of health insurance with government intervention/participation as needed. Choice C is incorrect because government regulation does not allow higher premiums for pre-existing conditions; in fact, that is one of the law's key prohibitions. Since the correct answer is B, this makes choice D irrelevant.

13. B. This answer is correct because vision care is not covered for adults but is provided as an add-on option to basic plans. Answer A is incorrect because basic plans do not cover vision care for adults. Choice C is incorrect because vision plans do not have to be purchased from a different company altogether or even from a different plan. Since there are options that allow supplementary vision plans, choice D is also incorrect.

14. A. The statement is not true because vision care for adults is not included under basic health insurance. Medicaid and Medicare cover essential health benefits for the most part, but this is not considered one of them. Answer B is incorrect because vision care for adults is not included under other basic health insurance. Choice C is not correct because eyeglasses and contacts are not considered essential medical treatments. Answer D is incorrect since choice A is correct.

15. B. The correct answer is "false" because vision insurance plans will not be made mandatory and therefore will not be subsidized (as of July 2013). Answer A is incorrect because it says that subsidies will cover vision insurance for adults. Answer C is incorrect because for

the most part vision care coverage is not situational and is based on whether the patient is an adult or a child.

16. C. The correct answer is 50 percent. This means that with proper care, half of all cases of vision impairment or blindness can be prevented. Choices A and B are too low, and answer D is too high.

17. D. This answer is correct because vision health typically varies depending on demographics and availability of resources. Answer A is incorrect because states have dissimilar population demographics, leading to differences in vision health issues. Choice B is incorrect because ocular health varies across racial groups for genetic or environmental reasons. Answer C is also incorrect because aging typically affects eyesight.

18. D. Glaucoma is a pressure buildup in the eye that can cause blindness if untreated. Answers A and B are incorrect because glaucoma is neither near-sightedness nor far-sightedness. Choice C is incorrect because tunnel vision is only a symptom of glaucoma, along with sharp pain.

19. B. Preventing glaucoma is important because it is a prime example of how early care can help save vision. Though glaucoma is preventable, it is one of the most common reasons for vision loss. Thus preventive vision care is imperative. Answer A is incorrect because glaucoma is preventable. Answers C and D are incorrect because Medicare covers glaucoma screening; however, treatment is another issue and is not necessarily covered.

20. D. The right choice is "All of the above" because all of the factors mentioned in A, B, and C are high-risk factors as outlined by the Centers for Medicare and Medicaid Services. Besides age, family history, medical history, and race are risk factors for glaucoma.

Sources

Questions 1, 2: HealthCare.gov,. Essential Health Benefits. Retrieved 29 September 2013, from https://www.healthcare.gov/glossary/essential-health-benefits/

Questions 1, 2, 3, 4: Sibson Consulting,. (2010). Capital checkup. Retrieved 29 September 2013, from http://www.sibson.com/publications/HCRI/dec2010DV.pdf

Question 4: Segalco.com,. (2012). Essential Health Benefits Proposal Presents Challenges for Plan Sponsors | Segal. Retrieved 5 September 2014, from http://www.segalco.com/publications-and-resources/multiemployer-publications/capital-checkup/archives/?id=1813

Questions 5, 6, 7: Ameritas, S. (2013). 10 Essential Facts About the Affordable Care Act, Dental and Vision Benefits | BenefitsPro. Benefitspro.com. Retrieved 29 September 2013, from http://www.benefitspro.com/2013/04/23/10-essential-facts-about-the-affordable-care-act-d

Question 5, 6, 7, 8: Washington Post,. (2012). Romney's right: Obamacare does not include dental care. Retrieved 29 September 2013, from http://www.washingtonpost.com/blogs/wonkblog/wp/2012/11/16/romneys-right-obamacare-does-not-include-dental-care/

Question 9: Prlog.org,. (2013). How Will Obamacare Effect Adult and Pediatric Dental Insurance Coverage? | PRLog. Retrieved 29 September 2013, from http://www.prlog.org/12137402-how-will-obamacare-effect-adult-and-pediatric-dental-insurance-coverage.html

Questions 10, 11, 12: RDH, R., & RDH, R. (2014). Obamacare and Dentistry. Adentmag.com. Retrieved 5 September 2014, from http://www.adentmag.com/obamacare-and-dentistry/

Questions 13, 14: Medicoverage.com,. (2013). Medicoverage - Affordable Health Insurance Quotes. Retrieved 5 September 2013, from http://www.medicoverage.com/health-insurance- blog/news/new-obamacare-health-plans-do-not-include-dental-vision

Question 15: Uniteforsight.org,. (2013). Eye Care Policy in the United States - Unite For Sight. Retrieved 29 September 2013, from http://www.uniteforsight.org/eye-care-policy/module1

Question 16, 17, 18: Cdc.gov,. (2012). Vision Surveillance in the US|Vision Health Initiative (VHI)|cdc.gov. Retrieved 5 September 2013, from http://www.cdc.gov/visionhealth/surveillance/index.htm

Questions 16, 17, 18: Chou, C., Barker, L., Crews, J., Primo, S., Zhang, X., & Elliott, A. et al. (2012). Disparities in Eye Care Utilization Among the United States Adults With Visual Impairment: Findings From the Behavioral Risk Factor Surveillance System 2006-2009. American Journal Of Ophthalmology, 154(6), 45--52.

Questions 18, 19, 20: Boyd, K. (2013). What Is Glaucoma? - Eye M.D.- approved information from EyeSmart. Geteyesmart.org. Retrieved 29 September 2013, from http://www.geteyesmart.org/eyesmart/diseases/glaucoma/

CHAPTER 5

Dental and Eye Care under ObamaCare: Part 2

Introduction to the chapter: This second chapter on dental and eye care under ObamaCare will address the concept of this treatment and interpret data on the characteristics of individuals most and least likely to obtain such care under the law.

Objective of the chapter: The chapter will offer a basic understanding of dental and eye care and provide common vocabulary used in these settings. Readers will learn, for instance, the basic difference between an optician and an optometrist, and between an optometrist and an ophthalmologist, in terms of the services they provide. Numeric data will familiarize readers with major issues concerning dental and eye care. As they navigate the health plans under ObamaCare, readers should easily understand the language of dental and ocular medicine, facilitating access to affordable care.

Hamisu Salihu, MD, PhD

The following graph shows by age group the percentage of the US population that visited a dentist within the previous year. Use this graph to answer questions 1 and 2.

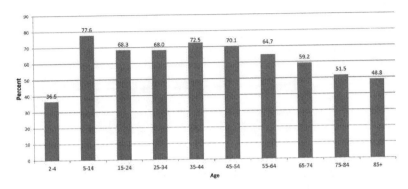

Source: Adapted from The Third National Health and Nutrition Examination Survey (NHANES III) 1988–1994, National Center for Health Statistics, Centers for Disease Control and Prevention

1. Which of the following most accurately represents the above data?

   a. The people who most commonly visit the dentist are those ages two to four.
   b. The people least likely to visit the dentist are those older than eighty-five.
   c. People around age forty are most likely to see the dentist.
   d. Older children and teenagers are most likely to visit the dentist.

2. Which of the following most accurately represents the above data?

   a. The people least likely to visit the dentist are those ages two to four.
   b. The people who most commonly visit the dentist are those older than eighty-five.
   c. People around age forty are the most likely to see the dentist.
   d. People in their twenties are the most likely to visit the dentist.

The following is a graph showing by demographics the percentage of the US population that visited a dentist within the past year. Use this to answer questions 3, 4, and 5.

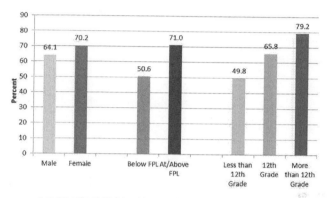

Source: Adapted from the Third National Health and Nutrition Examination Survey (NHANES III) 1988-1994, National Center for Health Statistics, Centers for Disease Control and Prevention

Note: "Education" represents the education of the head of the household for persons under eighteen; otherwise, it represents the education of the individual person. *FPL* stands for "Federal Poverty Level."

3. Which of the following most accurately represents the above data about sex and going to the dentist?

    a. Males and females go to the dentist at about the same frequency.
    b. Males go to the dentist more frequently.
    c. Females go to the dentist more frequently.
    d. All females go to the dentist.

4. Which of the following most accurately represents the above data about the federal poverty level?

    a. Those at or above this level have a higher dentist-visit rate.
    b. Those below this level have a higher dentist-visit rate.
    c. Those below the federal poverty level and those above it have roughly the same percentage of dentist visits.
    d. Only about half of all people in America go to the dentist.

5. Which of the following statements most accurately reflects the above data about education levels?

   a. Education does not seem to correlate with dental visits.
   b. Those below the federal poverty level and those above it have roughly the same percentage of dentist visits.
   c. There is a positive correlation between years of education and dental visits.
   d. Only about half of all people in America are educated past the high school level.

The following is a graph showing eye care estimates for American adults at high risk for serious vision loss versus those at low risk. Use this to answer questions 6, 7, and 8.

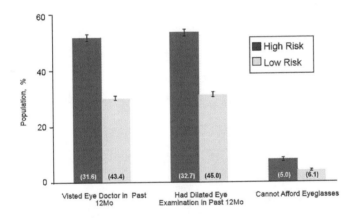

Data Source: 2002 National Health Interview Survey
Note: the numbers at the bottom of the column are in millions.

6. Which of the following statements is true?

    a. More than 20 percent of the combined high- and low-risk population cannot afford eyeglasses.
    b. Those at low risk typically have more eye care visits.
    c. Those at high risk typically have more eye care visits.
    d. More than 40 percent of the population did not go for eye care visits in the previous twelve months.

7. Which of the following statements is true?

    a. Thirty-two percent of the high-risk adult population has been to the eye doctor.
    b. Fifty percent of the high-risk adult population has been to the eye doctor.
    c. Thirty percent of the high-risk adult population has been to the eye doctor.
    d. Five percent of the high-risk adult population has been to the eye doctor.

8. Which of the following statements is true?

    a. More people showed up for eye dilation exams than for eye doctor visits.
    b. Fewer people showed up for eye dilation exams than for eye doctor visits.
    c. The same number of people showed up for eye dilation exams and for eye doctor visits.
    d. None of the above is correct.

The following chart is a commonly used eye exam device (called Snellen's Chart) that allows optometrists to assess a patient's eyesight. The chart is usually read from a distance of twenty feet. Use it for questions 9 and 10.

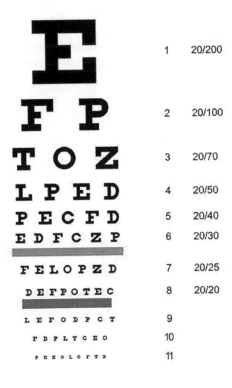

9. If Jimmy has trouble reading the letters on the sixth row, which of the following best represents his vision?

    a. 20/50
    b. 20/40
    c. 20/30
    d. 20/20

10. To have "perfect vision," which of the following row numbers must you be able to read past?

    a. Eighth row
    b. Seventh row
    c. Sixth row
    d. Fifth row

11. What is the best description of an optometrist?

    a. An eye doctor
    b. A person who fills eye care prescriptions
    c. A dental examiner
    d. An eye examiner

12. What is the best description of an ophthalmologist?

    a. An eye doctor
    b. A person who fills eye care prescriptions
    c. A dental examiner
    d. An eye examiner

13. What is the primary difference between an optometrist and an ophthalmologist?

    a. The ability to write prescriptions
    b. One is an M.D., while the other is a D.O.
    c. The services they offer
    d. There is little difference; one is just a more advanced form of the other.

14. What is an optician?

    a. An eye doctor
    b. A person who fills eye prescriptions
    c. A dental examiner
    d. An eye examiner

15. What is a cause of near-sightedness?

    a. Stress
    b. Genetics
    c. Both A and B
    d. None of the above

16. What is the symptom of far-sightedness?

    a. You focus on an object better close up.
    b. You cannot focus on a nearby object, and the image appears blurred.
    c. You can focus on nearby objects better than most people can.
    d. None of the above

17. The retina is located at the back of the eye and serves as a screen for the projection passing through the lens. An image is formed when light rays converge at one point. When light rays do not converge on the retina, a normal image is not formed. An impairment in the refraction of light rays coming from an object is associated with a number of eyesight disorders. Which of the following choices correctly match up the disorder with the point at which the light rays converge?

    a. Myopia: behind the retina
    b. Far-sightedness: before the retina
    c. Far-sightedness: the rays never converge
    d. Far-sightedness: behind the retina

18. What is a pupil?

    a. A black hole in the center of the eye
    b. A black spot in the center of the eye
    c. A colorful ring around the iris
    d. The clear, dome-shaped surface that covers the front of the eye

19. What does it mean to dilate the pupils?

    a. To make the pupils smaller to allow more light
    b. To make the pupils smaller to allow less light
    c. To make the pupils larger to allow more light
    d. To make the pupils larger to allow less light

20. Why do eye examiners dilate the pupils?

    a. To help people see better
    b. To allow more light to fall on the back of the eye for examination
    c. To reduce patient sensitivity to light
    d. None of the above

Answers

1. D. Older children and teenagers are the most likely to visit the dentist; the highest bar represents the five through fourteen age group. It has the top percentage of dentist attendees in the population. Answer A is incorrect because those ages two to four are the least likely to visit the dentist; only 36.5 percent of them saw a dentist during the period under study. Answer B is incorrect because the second least likely group is those older than eighty-five, with only a 48.8 percent attendance rate. Choice C is incorrect because people around forty, the group thirty-five to forty-four, are only the second most likely group to visit the dentist.

2. A. The correct answer is that the least likely group of people to see the dentist are those two to four years old; only 36.5 percent of them got dental care in a given year. Answer B is incorrect because the second least likely group is those older than eighty-five, with only a 48.8 percent attendance rate. Choice C is incorrect because those around forty, the group thirty-five to forty-four, are just the second most likely to visit the dentist. Answer D is incorrect because people in their twenties do not have the highest dentist attendance rate.

3. C. Females are more likely than males to go to the dentist; according to the graph, 70 percent of females visit the dentist compared with 64 percent of males. Answer A is incorrect because of the six-percentage-point difference between the groups. Choice B is incorrect because males get dental care less frequently. Answer D is wrong because the data do not say that all females go to the dentist, simply that more females go compared with males.

4. A. The correct answer is that those above the federal poverty level have a higher percentage of dentist visits; 71 percent of people above the level go to the dentist compared with 51 percent of people below the poverty line. Answer B is exactly the opposite of the correct

answer. Choice C is also incorrect because it says that those above and below the poverty level have the same percentage of dentist visits. Answer D is irrelevant because it does not refer to the federal poverty level and proposes a statement that is not directly verifiable from the given data.

5. C. The correct answer is that there is a positive correlation between years of education and dental visits; only 50 percent of those with less than a high school education saw a dentist within the period under study, whereas those who had more than a high school education averaged an attendance rate of 80 percent. Answer A is incorrect because it says that there is no correlation between education and dental visits. Choice B is incorrect because it says that education does not affect dental visits. Answer D is incorrect because it is not based on any evidence from the graph.

6. C. The correct answer is that those at higher risk show up more frequently for eye examinations. This is demonstrated by the longer blue bar (high risk) in all three scenarios. Answer A is incorrect because less than 15 percent of the combined high-risk and low-risk populations cannot afford eyeglasses, which is less than 20 percent. Choice B is incorrect because those at low risk do not show up for eye care as often as the high-risk group. Answer D is incorrect because no data from the graph supports the suggested conclusion.

7. B. The correct answer is that half of the high-risk population visited the eye doctor in the year studied. Answer A is incorrect because it gives the actual number (thirty-two million) as a percentage (32 percent). Answer C is incorrect because 30 percent of the low-risk, not the high-risk, population went to the eye doctor. Choice D is incorrect because 5 percent is much lower than the actual percentage of high-risk people who visited the eye doctor.

8. A. Add up the numbers from both bars (blue and yellow) for each category, and you find a difference of about 2.5 million favoring those who had an eye exam during which their pupils were dilated. Answer B is incorrect because it says the opposite. Choice C is incorrect because there is a significant difference between the two categories being compared. Answer D is incorrect.

9. B. The correct answer is that Jimmy has 20/40 vision. This is a distance chart, and to have a certain vision, it is necessary to read past a row correctly and without difficulty. Even if Jimmy has trouble reading the letters in row six, that means he made it past row five. Answer A is incorrect because it corresponds to row four instead of row five. Choice C is incorrect because it corresponds to row six instead of row five. Answer D is incorrect because it corresponds to row eight instead of row five.

10. A. To have "perfect vision," one must score 20/20. The chart shows which row corresponds to each scale of vision. In this case, 20/20 lies on the eighth row, and so it is necessary to be able to read past the eighth row in order to have "perfect vision." Answer B is incorrect because row seven corresponds to 20/25. Choice C is incorrect because row six corresponds to 20/30. Answer D is incorrect because row five corresponds to 20/40.

11. A. An optometrist is an eye doctor who specializes in eye examination and vision care. Although optometrists are not medical doctors, they are doctors of optometry. Answer A is correct because optometrists are eye doctors. Choice B is incorrect because people who fill eye prescriptions and make glasses are known as opticians. Answer C is incorrect because dental examiners are either dentists or orthodontists, not optometrists. Answer D is incorrect because eye examiner is not as specific as eye doctor, which is what optometrists are.

12. A. An ophthalmologist is an eye doctor who specializes in total eye care and medical problems related to the eye. Ophthalmologists are medical doctors. This makes answer A correct. Choice B is incorrect because people who fill eye prescriptions and make glasses are known as opticians. Answer C is incorrect because dental examiners are either dentists or orthodontists, not optometrists. Answer D is incorrect because eye examiner is not as specific as eye doctor, which is what ophthalmologists are.

13. C. There is one difference between optometrists and ophthalmologists, and that is the field that they cover. Optometrists provide vision care, while ophthalmologists deal with total eye care. Answer A is incorrect because both of them can write prescriptions. Choice B is incorrect because the ophthalmologist is usually an M.D. (medical doctor), while an optometrist is an O.D. (doctor of optometry), not a D.O. (doctor of osteopathy). Answer D is incorrect because there is a difference between the services optometrists and ophthalmologists offer.

14. B. An optician is a person who fills eye prescriptions and calibrates lenses to fit the prescription; this makes choice B correct. Answer A is incorrect because opticians are not doctors; optometrists and ophthalmologists are doctors. Answer C is incorrect because dental examiners are either dentists or orthodontists, not opticians. Choice D is incorrect because an optician does not examine the eye but makes instruments based on the optometrist's prescription.

15. C. The correct answer is that both stress and genetics cause near-sightedness. Answers A and B are correct, so the right answer is C because it includes both.

16. B. Far-sightedness is the inability to see (or to focus on) nearby objects well. The image of the object on the retina is blurry. Answer B best expresses this definition. Choice A is incorrect because it describes myopia, or near-sighted vision, and the affected individuals see (or

focus on) nearby objects well but find distant objects blurry. Answer C is incorrect because those with far-sighted vision cannot focus on nearby objects. Answer D is incorrect.

17. D. Far-sightedness exists when the light focuses behind the retina. Answer A is incorrect because it refers to myopia, a disorder in which the light rays converge behind the retina, a definition for far-sightedness. Choice B is incorrect because with far-sightedness, the rays converge behind the retina. Answer C is incorrect because the rays converge. The only time they wouldn't converge would be if the light rays were parallel, but because of the nature of the lens, all light coming through it bends and so there will be a point of convergence.

18. A. The pupil is a black hole in the center of the eye. Its purpose is to allow light to reach the retina at the back of the eye so that an image is formed. Answer B is incorrect because the pupil is a hole and not a spot. Choice C is incorrect because the colorful ring in the eye is known as the iris, which controls the size of the pupil. Answer D is also incorrect because the clear, dome-shaped surface that covers the front of the eye is the cornea.

19. C. *Dilate* means to open up. As the pupil gets larger, more light can pass through the larger hole. Answer A is incorrect because it says that dilating the eye makes the pupil smaller. The same applies to choice B. Answer D is incorrect because it says that making the pupil bigger allows less light to enter.

20. B. Eye examiners dilate pupils to allow more light to hit the back of the eye. This makes it easier to see what is going on inside the eye. One of the effects of dilating pupils is an increased sensitivity to light; the pupils essentially let in all light instead of limiting it. Answer A is incorrect because dilating the pupil does not help people see better. Answer C is incorrect because dilating the pupil actually increases the patient's sensitivity to light. Choice D is also incorrect.

Sources

Questions 1, 2, 3, 4, 5: Drc.hhs.gov,. (2002). 7.1 Delivery of Dental Services Annual Report - NIDCR/CDC Dental, Oral and Craniofacial Data Resource Center (DRC). Retrieved 17 October 2013, from http://drc.hhs.gov/report/7_1.htm

Questions 6, 7, 8: Cdc.gov,. (2009). CDC - Vision Health Initiative (VHI) - Publications: Use of Eye Care Services among American Adults. Retrieved 17 October 2013, from http://www.cdc.gov/visionhealth/publications/eyecare.htm

Questions 9, 10: I-see.org,. (2009). Eye Charts. Retrieved 17 October 2013, from http://www.i-see.org/eyecharts.html

Questions 11, 12, 13, 14: Webmd.com,. (2014). Eye Doctors: Optometrists and Ophthalmologists. Retrieved 5 September 2014, from http://www.webmd.com/eye-health/eye-doctors-optometrists-ophthalmologists

Question 15: Aoa.org,. (2014). Myopia (Nearsightedness). Retrieved 5 September 2014, from http://www.aoa.org/patients-and-public/eye-and-vision-problems/glossary-of-eye-and-vision-conditions/myopia?sso=y

Question 16, 17: Nlm.nih.gov,. (2014). Normal, nearsightedness, and farsightedness: MedlinePlus Medical Encyclopedia Image. Retrieved 5 September 2014, from http://www.nlm.nih.gov/medlineplus/ency/imagepages/19511.htm

Questions 18, 19: Exploratorium: the museum of science, art and human perception,. (2014). Pupil: Life Science, Perception & Light Activity | Exploratorium Science Snacks. Retrieved 3 September 2014, from http://www.exploratorium.edu/snacks/pupil/

Question 20: Nei.nih.gov,. (2014). Why does my doctor put drops in my eyes to dilate my pupils for an exam? Eye on NEI, Ask the Doctor, National Eye Institute [NEI]. Retrieved 18 August 2014, from http://www.nei.nih.gov/eyeonnei/askthedoctor/archive/0210.asp

CHAPTER 6

ObamaCare: Opposing Viewpoints

Introduction to the chapter: When implementation of ObamaCare began, misleading statements for and against provisions of the law flooded the media.

Objective of the chapter: This chapter will enable readers to understand the basic principles and impact of ObamaCare at the individual and national levels. For instance, this section will examine the law's impact on the cost of health insurance and on the independence of physicians in managing patients to provide optimal care.

This set of questions refers to criticisms of ObamaCare. While some of the criticisms involve legitimate concerns, others are unfounded and, in many cases, misleading. See if you can distinguish fact from fiction.

1. ObamaCare will prevent physicians from opening up their own practices.

    a. True
    b. False. Physicians will not be affected by ObamaCare policies.
    c. False. ObamaCare may require more paperwork from physicians, but it will not prohibit opening private clinical enterprises.

2. ObamaCare will not allow flexibility between the patient and the doctor in determining the best treatment.

   a. True, because there is always only one viable treatment for any given illness
   b. True, because the government will decide exactly what course of treatment is to be followed for a given illness and will determine the role of the treating doctor
   c. False, because the doctor will still be able to offer the level of care most appropriate for the patient

3. There will be a tax on the sale of medical equipment.

   a. True. It will be 40 percent of the sale price of the equipment.
   b. True. It will be less than 5 percent of the sale price of the equipment.
   c. False, because such a tax is not constitutional.
   d. False. Such a tax is constitutional but is not in effect.

4. Patients will have to pay for the excise tax on medical equipment.

   a. True
   b. False. The providers using the equipment will have to pay for the medical excise tax.
   c. False. Importers and manufacturers will have to report and pay the costs related to the excise tax on medical equipment.

5. The government has predicted that the cost of health insurance will come down, but recent trends suggest a likely increase.

   a. True. While the Department of Health and Human Services predicted costs would decline, the requirement for essential health benefits under ObamaCare would potentially make even the cheapest plans more expensive.

b. False. Government regulation will bring a decrease.
c. True. Everyone knows that the cost of health insurance is not going to come down at all.

The following set of graphs compares bronze premiums for a woman and a man, both twenty-seven. Numbers shown for the states represent percentage increases in premiums.

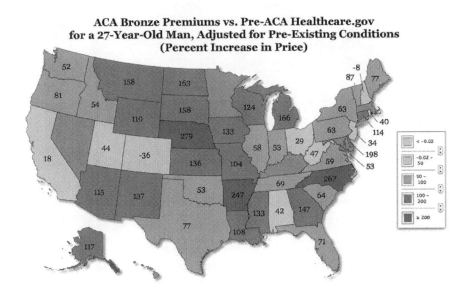

Forbes,. (2013). *Double Down: Obamacare Will Increase Avg. Individual-Market Insurance Premiums By 99% For Men, 62% For Women*. Retrieved 16 August 2014, from http://www.forbes.com/sites/theapothecary/2013/09/25/double-down-obamacare-will-increase-avg-individual-market-insurance-premiums-by-99-for-men-62-for-women/

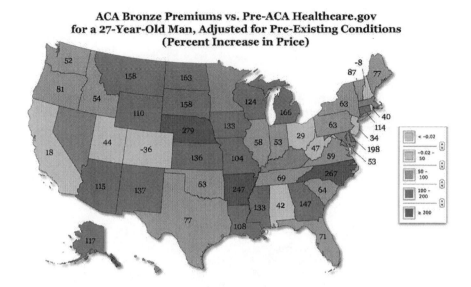

Forbes,. (2013). *Double Down: Obamacare Will Increase Avg. Individual-Market Insurance Premiums By 99% For Men, 62% For Women*. Retrieved 16 August 2014, from http://www.forbes.com/sites/theapothecary/2013/09/25/double-down-obamacare-will-increase-avg-individual-market-insurance-premiums-by-99-for-men-62-for-women/

6. Based on the charts above, which of the following statements is true?

   a. All states will see an increase in the price of health insurance for men.
   b. Few states will see an increase in health insurance rates.
   c. No states will see an increase in health insurance premiums.
   d. None of the above

7. Based on the charts above, which of the following statements is true?

   a. The gray states represent those for which there is no change in health insurance prices.

b. The gray states represent those in which there is no health exchange.
c. The gray states represent those with fewer than a million people.
d. The gray states represent those for which the federal government did not release information.

8. Based on the charts above, which of the following statements is true?

a. Men seem to have the advantage regarding health insurance prices.
b. Women seem to have the advantage regarding health insurance prices.
c. Women and men face the same situation regarding health insurance prices.
d. Children have the biggest advantage regarding health insurance prices.

The following set of graphs compares bronze premiums for a woman and a man, both forty. Numbers shown for the states represent percentage increases in premiums.

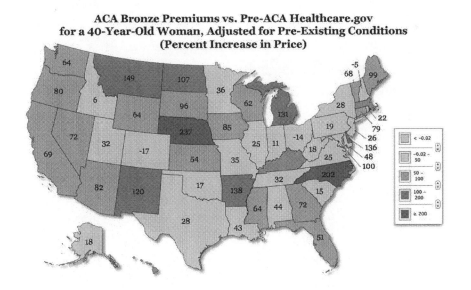

Forbes,. (2013). *Double Down: Obamacare Will Increase Avg. Individual-Market Insurance Premiums By 99% For Men, 62% For Women.* Retrieved 16 August 2014, from http://www.forbes.com/sites/theapothecary/2013/09/25/double-down-obamacare-will-increase-avg-individual-market-insurance-premiums-by-99-for-men-62-for-women/

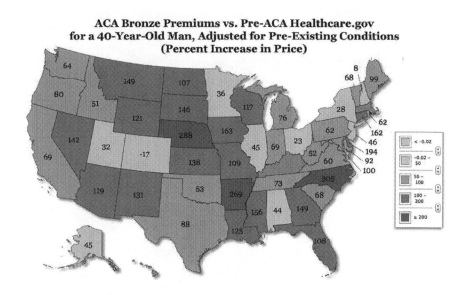

Forbes,. (2013). *Double Down: Obamacare Will Increase Avg. Individual-Market Insurance Premiums By 99% For Men, 62% For Women.* Retrieved 16 August 2014, from http://www.forbes.com/sites/theapothecary/2013/09/25/double-down-obamacare-will-increase-avg-individual-market-insurance-premiums-by-99-for-men-62-for-women/

9. Based on the charts above, which of the following statements is true?

   a. Men seem to have the advantage regarding health insurance prices.
   b. Women seem to have the advantage regarding health insurance prices.
   c. Women and men face the same situation regarding health insurance prices.

d. Children have the biggest advantage regarding health insurance prices.

10. Based on the charts above, which of the following statements is true?

    a. The first two charts differ from the last two concerning the age of the individuals.
    b. The first two charts differ from the last two concerning the type of insurance.
    c. The charts differ. The first two are projected for October 2013, while the last two are projected for October 2014.
    d. The first two charts do not differ from the last two.

11. Based on the charts above, which of the following correctly matches a state with the percentage increase in price for women?

    a. Florida: 51%
    b. Texas: 17%
    c. New York: 62%
    d. Alabama: 156%

12. Based on the charts above, which of the following correctly matches a state with the percentage increase in price for men?

    a. Florida: 69%
    b. New York: 28%
    c. California: 108%
    d. North Carolina: 60%

13. The Independent Payment Advisory Board will reduce coverage.

    a. True, because one way of reducing health care costs to the government is a reduction of coverage

b. True, because the board is empowered under ObamaCare to do anything to reduce costs
c. False, because the board seeks to reduce the cost to the government, but without decreasing coverage

14. Millions of employees with stable insurance may lose coverage because it does not comply with new regulations.

    a. True, because a few big companies were no longer allowed to stay in the market, and as a result all of their customers were left without insurance
    b. False. Everyone who has insurance will continue to have it.
    c. False. Millions is an exaggeration.

15. Which of the following states did the scenario above affect?

    a. California
    b. New Jersey
    c. Missouri
    d. All of the above

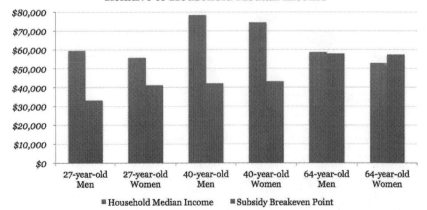

Forbes,. (2013). *Double Down: Obamacare Will Increase Avg. Individual-Market Insurance Premiums By 99% For Men, 62% For Women*. Retrieved 16 August 2014, from http://www.forbes.com/sites/theapothecary/2013/09/25/double-down-obamacare-will-increase-avg-individual-market-insurance-premiums-by-99-for-men-62-for-women/

16. Based on the charts above, which of the following statements is true?

    a. Government subsidies are most useful to twenty-seven-year-old men.
    b. Government subsidies are most useful to forty-year-old women.
    c. Government subsidies are most useful to forty-year-old men.
    d. Government subsidies are most useful to sixty-four-year-old women.

17. Based on the charts above, which of the following statements is false?

    a. The household median income for forty-year-old men is almost $80,000.
    b. The household median income for forty-year-old women is almost $75,000.
    c. The subsidy break-even point is $40,000 for both forty-year-old men and women.
    d. None of the above

18. Based on the charts above, the greatest difference between median household income and the subsidy break-even point is in which group?

    a. Forty-year-old men
    b. Forty-year-old women
    c. Twenty-seven-year-old men
    d. Twenty-seven-year-old women

19. If an individual receives a subsidy when he/she applied for his/her health insurance, it is in his/her best interest not to receive a promotion or pay increase during that year.

    a. True. It is generally discouraged for individuals to secure additional income in an effort to avoid end of the year penalties
    b. False. The individual can contact Healthcare.gov or the state exchange to update their information and avoid any potential penalty
    c. False. Subsidies are only calculated by the individual's income at the time of the application and are not influenced by changes in income after the application is approved
    d. False. Subsidies are only provided to families, not individuals, therefore the scenario does not apply

20. If it is determined that a family has received more tax credits than they were supposed to, they may face the following consequences at the end of the year:

    a. A reduction in their tax return.
    b. A lien or levy to collect penalties.
    c. Writing a check to the IRS to cover repayment.
    d. All of the above
    e. None of the above. Currently, there are no established consequences for this scenario.

Answers

1. C. The answer is "false." ObamaCare may require more paperwork from physicians, but it will not prohibit opening private practices. Thus. Answer A is incorrect. Choice B is incorrect because physicians will be affected by ObamaCare policies.

2. C. The correct answer is that doctors will be able to offer the care most appropriate for patients. Answer A is incorrect because it implies a single treatment pathway for every illness. A medical problem typically has more than one solution, and a doctor will determine what needs to be done to provide optimal care. Choice B is incorrect because it says that under ObamaCare the government will decide which treatment must be given. This would lower the quality of health care by eliminating a personalized approach that takes into account patients' varying needs. The take-home message: ObamaCare does not dictate to physicians which treatment must be delivered.

3. B. ObamaCare imposes an excise tax on medical equipment. This makes choices C and D incorrect because they describe the statement as false. Answer A is incorrect because 40 percent is too high. The excise tax on medical equipment will be about 2.5 percent of the sale price. B is the correct answer because it says that the tax will be less than 5 percent. [*As of August 2014, there is bipartisan support in both chambers of Congress to repeal the excise tax, however a bill has yet been passed to implement the repeal].

4. C. The tax on medical equipment is a cost that must be paid by the importer or the manufacturer, and not by the patient. Answer A is incorrect because it says that the patient will have to pay the tax. Providers will not have to pay the tax on medical equipment because they are not the manufacturers or the importers. Thus choice B is also incorrect.

5. A. Health insurance costs may increase. The key word is *may*. Answer A is correct because while the Department of Health and Human Services predicted lower costs, the forecast was made in comparison with expected costs several years ago. This perhaps explains the disparity between the observed versus the expected health insurance costs following the implementation of ObamaCare. In addition, many people have basic plans, while ObamaCare requires "minimal" plans that provide more coverage and are therefore more expensive. This may cause an initial uptick in health care costs as well. Choices B and C are incorrect, not only because they say that the statement is false but because they exclude the possibility that costs may increase.

6. D. The answer is "None of the above" because the optimal choice is not offered. The question asks for the number of states that will see increases in health insurance rates; these are shown by red or peach colors. Answer A is incorrect because not all of the states will see increases; the ones shown in blue will experience decreases. Choice B is incorrect because it says that few states will see rate increases. Answer C is incorrect because it says that none of the states will see increases, when in fact most will.

7. D. The chart explains the predictions for increases or decreases in health care exchange prices. The question asks what areas with no color represent. The correct answer is that there is no information for those without color. For these states, the Department of Health and Human Services did not release information. Answer A is incorrect because states with no change are shown in tan with a zero percent increase. This is the case, for example, with Pennsylvania and the information on women's rates. Answer B is incorrect because health exchanges will operate in every state, but they can be run by the state government, the federal government, or a combination of the two. The chart says nothing about the population, and this makes choice C incorrect.

8. B. The correct answer is that on average, women will see a smaller increase in health insurance rates than will men. Answer A is incorrect because it suggests that men have the advantage. Choice C is incorrect because it implies that men and women will find insurance equally expensive. Answer D is incorrect because the chart does not refer to children.

9. B. The correct answer is that on average, women will see a smaller increase in health insurance rates than will men. Answer A is incorrect because it suggests that men have the advantage. Choice C is incorrect because it implies that men and women will find insurance equally expensive. Answer D is incorrect because the chart does not refer to children.

10. A. The correct answer is that the two sets of charts differ based on the age of the people examined for policies. The first two charts are for twenty-seven-year-old adults, while the last two are for forty-year-old adults. Answer B is incorrect because both sets examine bronze plans. Choice C is incorrect because both sets are based on this health exchange. Answer D is incorrect because the two charts contain different information.

11. A. The only state matched up correctly with its increase in the cost of health care for women is Florida with a 51 percent rise over its current price. Answer B is incorrect because Texas will see an 88 percent increase, not a 17 percent rise. Choice C is incorrect because New York will see a much smaller increase, 28 percent instead of 62 percent. Answer D is incorrect because Alabama will see a 44 percent increase, unlike Mississippi, which will see a 156 percent rise.

12. B. The only state matched up correctly with its increase in insurance rates for men is New York at a 28 percent hike. Answer A is incorrect because Florida faces a much higher increase than 69 percent; it is 108 percent. Answer C is incorrect because California will see a much

lower increase than 108 percent; it is 69 percent. North Carolina faces a much higher increase than mentioned, 308 percent instead of 60 percent.

13. C. The Independent Payment Advisory Board is a government agency that seeks to reduce unnecessary health care spending. One of the key criteria, however, is that the board's decisions must not affect health care quality or coverage. Answer A is incorrect because it implies that there is no option but to reduce coverage, which runs contrary to the fundamental tenets of ObamaCare. Choice B is incorrect because although the board will typically seek to reduce excess spending, it will not do so to the detriment of coverage.

14. A. The correct answer is that because of coverage regulations some big insurance companies were no longer allowed to provide insurance. People covered by those companies lost their insurance policies. Choice B is incorrect because not everyone who has insurance will continue to have it. Answer C is incorrect because millions of people indeed lost coverage for this reason.

15. D. The correct answer is that the scenario above affected all three states mentioned in this question. At least 58,000 people in California lost their health insurance, 79,000 in Missouri, and 1.1 million in New Jersey. They were dropped by the same company in all three states.

16. D. Government subsidies are most useful to those whose household incomes fall below the subsidy break-even point. The only group that shows a median income under the break-even point is sixty-four-year-old women. This is choice D. For the most part, choices A, B, and C are incorrect. It would be foolish to make less money simply to be eligible for subsidies. Answers A, B, and C are represented in the blue bars, which show income well above that in the red bars, indicating that people in these groups would not benefit from incomes eligible for subsidies.

17. D. The correct answer is "None of the above" because all of the statements are true. The household median income for forty-year-old men is almost $80,000. The household median income for forty-year-old women is almost $75,000. Finally, the subsidy break-even point is the same for forty-year-old men and women: $40,000.

18. A. The correct answer is that for forty-year-old men there is roughly a $40,000 difference between household median income and the subsidy break-even point. Answer B is incorrect because there is about a $35,000 difference for forty-year-old women. Answers C and D are incorrect because the numbers are smaller: twenty-seven-year-old men show a difference of $25,000, and twenty-seven-year-old women show a difference of about $15,000.

19. B. The answer is False. Subsidies and tax credits are available to individuals and families with household incomes between 100 and 400 percent of the federal poverty level, taking into account several factors. If the yearly income exceeds the estimate provided when the individual/family applied for health insurance, perhaps due to a promotion or pay increase, the tax refund may be reduced or eliminated. To avoid this penalty, the individual or family should contact Healthcare.gov or the state health exchange to report the additional income. Reporting the additional income may result in the subsidy being reduced or the premiums being increased but reporting the additional income reduces the potential of being responsible for repayment at the end of the year. Therefore, answers A, C, and D are incorrect.

20. D. The correct answer is All of the above (D). If the individual's tax refund isn't sufficient to cover the repayment, the individual may have to write the IRS a check. Fortunately, the repayment amount the IRS can collect is capped for most individuals/families. In contrast to the penalties for those who remain uninsured, there is no limitation on collection efforts in situations where individuals received too big a tax credit; liens and levies may be used.

Sources

Questions 1. 2, 3, 4, 5, 6, 7, 8, 9, 10, 11, 16, 17, 18: Forbes,. (2013). *Double Down: Obamacare Will Increase Avg. Individual-Market Insurance Premiums By 99% For Men, 62% For Women*. Retrieved 16 August 2014, from http://www.forbes.com/sites/theapothecary/2013/09/25/double-down-obamacare-will-increase-avg-individual-market-insurance-premiums-by-99-for-men-62-for-women/

Questions 3, 4: Irs.gov,. (2014). *Medical Device Excise Tax: Frequently Asked Questions*. Retrieved 5 September 2014, from http://www.irs.gov/uac/Medical-Device-Excise-Tax:-Frequently-Asked-Questions

Questions 1, 2, 3, 4: PBS NewsHour,. (2013). *PBS NewsHour*. Retrieved 3 November 2013, from http://www.pbs.org/newshour/rundown/2013/09/how-will-the-obamacare-mandate-impact-you.html

Question 5: Holly Yan, C. (2013). *Government shutdown: Get up to speed in 20 questions*. CNN. Retrieved 3 November 2013, from http://www.cnn.com/2013/09/30/politics/government-shutdown-up-to-speed

Question 12: McClanahan, C. (2012). *What Is The Independent Medicare Advisory Board?*. Forbes. Retrieved 5 September 2014, from http://www.forbes.com/sites/carolynmcclanahan/2012/10/04/what-is-the-independent-medicare-advisory-board/

Question 13, 14: The Daily Caller,. (2013). *Ten states where Obamacare wipes out existing health care plans*. Retrieved 5 November 2013, from http://dailycaller.com/2013/09/28/ten-states-where-obamacare-wipes-out-existing-health-care-plans/

Question 19, 20: Cbsnews.com,. (2014). *How Obamacare subsidies could impact your tax refund*. Retrieved 17 September 2014, from http://www.cbsnews.com/news/how-obamacare-subsidies-could-impact-your-tax-refund/

CHAPTER 7

ObamaCare and the Business Environment

Introduction to the chapter: The chapter describes health plan options, discusses the definition and characteristics of a small business under ObamaCare, and explains how these businesses operate and shop on the health exchange market.

Objective of the chapter: Readers will learn terms commonly used in the health care business environment and will discover what to purchase as they navigate the insurance exchange market. Finally, readers will learn metrics commonly used to describe small businesses, incentives offered to these businesses under ObamaCare, and where these businesses go to shop on the exchange market.

1. Which of the following statements gives a possible explanation as to why certain states have refused to participate in ObamaCare?

    a. They wanted to exercise states' rights.
    b. They hoped to avoid possible net losses to taxpayers.
    c. There is no profit incentive for them to participate.
    d. More than one of the above

2. Which of these statements provides a plausible explanation as to why certain people refused to participate in ObamaCare?

   a. Doing so would cost them more money annually.
   b. They feel that the program impinges on personal freedom.
   c. They may not need a health plan.
   d. All of the above

The questions that follow (3 to 10) are posed as a series of statements in a tabular format. These statements can be described by a single word from the third column of the table. Find the matching word and place it in column two against the correct statement.

Table 7.1: See how well you know the different types of health care providers and plans.

Statement descriptor	Answer	Matching word
3. Health insurance program that caters to the needs of those who are typically 65+ or disabled.		a. Bronze
4. Health insurance program that caters to the needs of those who are typically economically disadvantaged.		b. Gold
5. The health plan that covers about 80% of all medical costs.		c. HMO
6. The "average" health plan that has important benefits.		d. Medicaid

7. The health plan that is subject to an excise tax unless an exemption is made.		e. Medicare
8. A health plan that contracts with a network of healthcare providers; but offers the flexibility of going outside of the network.		f. Platinum
9. A health plan that is built for people who do not anticipate use of medical services.		g. PPO
10. A health plan that requires the patient to choose a doctor or specialist within the network.		h. Silver
		i. Diamond

The following questions concern businesses and the impact ObamaCare could have on them.

11. What are some of the characteristics that would qualify a firm as a small business?

    a. Having fewer than a thousand employees
    b. Making less than $1 million in annual profit
    c. Depends on the industry

12. What is the difference between revenue and profit?

    a. Revenue and profit are the same thing.
    b. Revenue is the sum total of money remaining after expenses are paid, while profit is the sum total made before expenses.

c. Profit is the sum total of money remaining after expenses are paid, while revenue is the sum total made before expenses are deducted.
d. None of the above

13. What percentage of all businesses are small businesses with fewer than fifty people?

    a. 96%
    b. 24%
    c. 83%
    d. 52%

14. What percentage of all people employed work for small businesses?

    a. 25%
    b. 50%
    c. 75%
    d. 99%

15. How will ObamaCare affect businesses with more than fifty employees?

    a. Require them to provide health insurance for their employees, assuming that revenue will cover the costs
    b. Require them to provide insurance for their employees but make it possible to finance the costs
    c. Not require them to provide insurance as long as they are small businesses
    d. Will not affect most of these small businesses

16. Which of the following describes the incentives for small businesses that are required to provide health insurance for their employees?

    a. Tax credits
    b. Discounts

c. Exemptions
d. More than one of the above

17. What criteria will help qualify businesses for tax credits?

    a. Fewer than twenty-five employees
    b. Paying for 50 percent of employee premiums
    c. Average annual wages under $50,000
    d. All of the above

18. Are nonprofit organizations also considered businesses?

    a. Yes, because they are classified as tax-exempt
    b. No, because they are charities
    c. Yes, because they aim to make profit
    d. No, because they do not make a profit

19. Who is responsible for enforcing health care policies?

    a. The federal government
    b. The states
    c. The police
    d. The Bureau of Health Enforcement

20. Is there a marketplace where small businesses can shop for coverage?

    a. No. There is no specific marketplace for small businesses; they have to use the regular health exchange.
    b. Yes. It is called the Small Business Health Options Program (SHOP).
    c. Yes. It is called the Marketplace for Health Insurance.
    d. It depends on whether a small business qualifies (using certain additional criteria) to participate in the online exchange for small businesses.

Answers

1. D. The correct answer is "More than one of the above" because two of the choices are correct. Answer A is correct because states that have refused to participate are exercising states' rights regardless of whether this yields victory. Choice B is also correct since ObamaCare will initially require some investment. The hope, however, is that the investment will eventually pay for itself. Answer C is incorrect because there are incentives to states participating in ObamaCare. Although profits are not anticipated at first, in the long run, they are expected from the investment. This makes choice C incorrect because it says that there is no profit incentive at all.

2. D. The correct answer is "All of the above." Answer A is correct because people who have plans without all of the essential health benefits will pay extra for new plans that require more coverage. . Choice B is correct because many people believe that it is unjust to be forced to buy health insurance. Answer C is also correct because perfectly healthy people may not currently need insurance. However, an unexpected accident could make the decision to go without insurance costly and unwise.

3. E. The correct answer is a program that insures those who are older or permanently disabled. Medicaid focuses on those who are economically disadvantaged but otherwise typically healthy. Medicare focuses on people sixty-five and up and those with specific permanent disabilities. Out of these options, Medicare best fits the description.

4. D. The correct answer is Medicaid, which focuses on those who are economically disadvantaged but otherwise typically healthy. Medicare focuses on individuals sixty-five and up and those with specific permanent disabilities. Out of these options, Medicaid best fits the description.

5. B. The correct answer is the gold plan. The choices listed are bronze, silver, gold, and platinum, the four types of health plans offered by private and public insurance entities. Bronze covers 60 percent of all medical expenses, silver covers 70 percent, gold covers 80 percent, and platinum covers 90 percent.

6. H. The choices for this question are bronze, silver, gold, and platinum. The percentages of coverage are detailed in the answer above. Silver plans may not include unnecessary medical procedures, but they cover the essential health benefits and offer more coverage. This is the "average" plan selected by most clients.

7. F. The correct answer is platinum. The other choices are bronze, silver, and gold. One reason platinum plans are taxed is because they are considered premium plans and are deemed unnecessary unless the patient is in a high-risk profession. Those who have platinum plans, but do not demonstrate a need for such a plan, will face a tax equaling 40 percent of the premium. Those holding these "Cadillac plans" can gain partial to full exemption from the tax.

8. G. The correct answer is a PPO. An HMO, the other choice, offers a network of health care providers. A patient will pay the full price for care outside of that network. A PPO offers a network of providers but allows the flexibility of visiting health care providers outside of the network.

9. A. The correct answer is bronze because it is the least expensive of the plans. The other options for this question are silver, gold, and platinum. For those who do not anticipate using medical services, the least costly plan would seem fitting.

10. C. The correct answer is HMO. There are two likely choices for this question, an HMO and a PPO. An HMO offers a network of health care providers, and care outside of that network costs almost full

price. A PPO offers a network of providers but allows the flexibility of seeing health care providers outside of the network at greater cost to the patient. The type of health plan mentioned in this problem is an HMO because the plan does not provide the flexibility of going outside of the network.

11. C. The answer is that it depends on the industry. That's because some industries demand more labor, depending on the type of work required. Answer A is incorrect because having a thousand employees means the business is large rather than small. Choice B is incorrect because profit is not generally used to gauge the size of a business. Answer D is incorrect because choice C is correct.

12. C. Revenue is the total influx of money before expenses, and profit is the money remaining after expenses have been paid. Since these are not the same, choice A is incorrect. Answer B says the opposite and therefore is also incorrect. Answer C correctly defines profit and revenue. This makes choice D incorrect.

13. A. The correct answer is 96 percent. Most small businesses have fewer than fifty employees. Answer B is incorrect because it is too low, and the same goes for choices C and D. Almost all businesses have fewer than fifty employees.

14. B. The answer is 50 percent. About half of all people employed in the United States work for small businesses. Choice A is half of the correct percentage. Answers C and D are too high.

15. B. The correct answer is that ObamaCare will affect small businesses because it requires companies with more than fifty workers to provide insurance. Choices C and D are incorrect because these companies have more than fifty employees and must offer insurance. Answer A is incorrect because it implies that small businesses will not receive help of any kind. Tax credits are among the benefits offered to small

businesses that provide health insurance to their workers. Note that the cap of fifty employees for small business under ObamaCare may change.

16. A. The correct answer is that small businesses providing health insurance to their employees will be offered tax credits as incentives. Answer B is incorrect because small businesses will not be offered discounts on health insurance, only the potentially lower prices resulting from market competition. Choice C is also incorrect because there are virtually no exemptions for small businesses required to provide insurance to their employees. Answer D is incorrect.

17. D. All the choices are correct because tax credits are meant to help businesses that provide insurance to employees. Answer A is correct because businesses with fewer than twenty-five employees qualify for tax credits. The same applies to businesses that pay 50 percent of employee health insurance premiums or have average annual wages under $50,000.

18. A. Nonprofit organizations are considered businesses that do not make profit. They may have revenue but must use that to further their goals. Because they do not make a profit, they qualify as tax-exempt businesses. Answer B is incorrect because although a nonprofit may be charitable, it is still considered a business. Choice C is incorrect since nonprofit organizations do not make a profit or distribute money as dividends. Answer D is incorrect. These organizations remain nonprofit since the revenues they generate are used to pursue their goals and are not distributed as profits or dividends.

19. B. The correct answer is that the state is responsible for enforcing health care laws. Since every state has its own, slightly different version of ObamaCare, enforcement occurs at the state level. Answer A is incorrect because it is not the federal government that enforces health care law. Choice C is incorrect because police are responsible

for enforcement of criminal law, and violation of health care policies does not fall under that category. Answer D is incorrect because the "Bureau of Health Enforcement" does not exist.

20. B. The correct answer is the Small Business Health Options Program, or SHOP. This special exchange marketplace for small businesses makes it easier for business owners to navigate plans and look for competitive prices. Answer A is incorrect because it denies the existence of an exchange. Answer C is incorrect because it names the exchange as the Marketplace for Health Insurance. Choice D is incorrect because all small businesses that wish to provide their employees with insurance are allowed to use the SHOP exchange without additional criteria.

Sources

Question 1: Pewstates.org,. (2013). *Stateline*. Retrieved 22 November 2013, from http://www.pewstates.org/projects/stateline/headlines/state-resistance-to-federal-government-goes-back-to-us-beginnings-85899499361

Question 1: Tanner, M. (2012). *Michael Tanner - The States Resist Obamacare. National Review Online*. Retrieved 20 November 2013, from http://www.nationalreview.com/articles/304729/states-resist-ObamaCare-michael-tanner

Questions 8, 10: Medicare.gov,. (2013). *Your Medicare coverage choices | Medicare.gov*. Retrieved 20 November 2013, from http://www.medicare.gov/sign-up-change-plans/decide-how-to-get-medicare/your-medicare-coverage-choices.html

Question 12: Tutor2u.net,. (2014). *GCSE Economics - Finance: Revenue and Profit*. Retrieved 25 November 2013, from http://www.tutor2u.net/economics/gcse/revision_notes/finance_revenue_profit.htm

Questions 11, 13, 14, 15, 16, 17, 18, 19, 20: Small Business Association Office of Advocacy,. (2012). *Frequently Asked Questions*. Retrieved 25 November 2013, from http://www.sba.gov/sites/default/files/FAQ_Sept_2012.pdf

CHAPTER 8

How the Health Exchange Works

Introduction to the chapter: The chapter begins with a brief discussion of how allowing broader competition in the health insurance markets will drive down premium rates. This is followed by an introduction to the health exchange site and what prospective clients can expect to see on the screenshot as they apply for health plans. As the government health exchange websites get better, the application format may change.

Objective of the chapter: The chapter's main goal is to show the reasoning behind the exchanges and how competition in the health insurance markets might increase affordability. The questions and answers in this chapter will give readers a better understanding of how the health exchange works.

1. What is people's major complaint when they try to enroll in health plans with insurance companies?

    a. The plans are not comprehensive enough.
    b. The plans are too cheap.
    c. The plans are not affordable.
    d. The plans cover too many unnecessary services.

2. What is the primary reason prices for health care plans were not dropping before ObamaCare?

   a. Few health insurance companies were participating in the markets.
   b. Too many health insurance companies were participating in the markets.
   c. The government did not regulate health insurance strictly enough.
   d. The government was overregulating health insurance.

3. Which of the following areas are most affected by high insurance costs under ObamaCare?

   a. Urban
   b. Suburban
   c. Military
   d. Rural

4. Which of the following is a correct statement?

   a. Health insurance companies are not concerned about losing money through their participation in ObamaCare.
   b. Hospitals are reluctant to lower prices for medical procedures.
   c. Both of the above are correct.
   d. None of the above is correct.

5. Another kind of health plan, known as a catastrophic plan, has become available. The plan's features include:

   a. High deductibles
   b. Low deductible
   c. High premiums
   d. Coverage of long-term hospital stays

6. Catastrophic health plans are good for people who:

    a. Have pre-existing conditions
    b. See the doctor frequently
    c. Have regular prescription drugs
    d. Cannot afford more coverage

7. Catastrophic health insurance plans do not provide coverage for preventive care.

    a. True
    b. False

8. Compared with other plans, which of the following statements is accurate about catastrophic health insurance plans?

    a. Monthly premiums may be higher.
    b. Annual deductibles may be lower.
    c. They will cover emergency room visits.
    d. They are perfect for people who will have another insurance plan in six to twelve months.

Bronze $10 Copay HMO	Estimated monthly premium for
Insurance Group A	Only you
HMO/Bronze	$146.58

Insurance Group B Basic	Estimated monthly premium for
Insurance Group B	Only you
PPO/Catastrophic	$186.24

Silver $10 Copay HMO	Estimated monthly premium for
Insurance Group A	Only you
HMO/Silver	$189.05

Insurance Group C Essential HSA	Estimated monthly premium for
Insurance Group C	Only you
EPO/Bronze	$189.24

9. On the chart above, which plan would be the cheapest if these were the only options available to you?

   a. The catastrophic plan
   b. Insurance Group A HMO bronze plan
   c. Insurance Group A HMO silver plan
   d. Insurance Group C EPO bronze plan

10. What is an EPO?

    a. Exclusive provider organization
    b. Environmental protection organization
    c. Exclusive parent option
    d. European Patient Office

11. Which is offering the cheapest non-HMO health plan?

    a. Insurance Group A
    b. Insurance Group B
    c. Insurance Group C
    d. None of the above

Scenario A: If I am a thirty-five-year-old woman seeking insurance, my information will look like this:

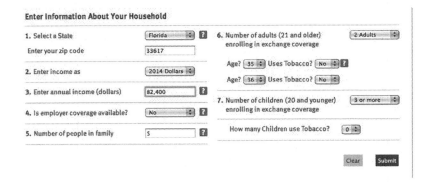

Hamisu Salihu, MD, PhD

My report will look like this:

RESULTS

The information below is about subsidized exchange coverage. Note that subsidies are only available for people purchasing coverage on their own in the exchange (not through an employer). Depending on your state's eligibility criteria, you or some members of your family may qualify for Medicaid.

Household income in 2014:	299% of poverty level
Maximum % of income you have to pay for the non-tobacco premium, if eligible for a subsidy:	9.47%
Health Insurance premium in 2014 (for a silver plan, before tax credit):	$9,938 per year
You could receive a government tax credit subsidy of up to:	$2,137 per year (which covers 22% of the overall premium)
Amount you pay for the premium:	$7,801 per year (which equals 9.47% of your household income and covers 78% of the overall premium)

12. The amount of money I will receive from the government to cover my health insurance is:

    a. 299 percent of the health insurance premium
    b. 87 percent of the health insurance premium
    c. 22 percent of the health insurance premium
    d. 10 percent of the health insurance premium

13. How many children do I have?

    a. One
    b. Two
    c. Three
    d. None

14. Do I have a husband?

    a. Possibly
    b. Absolutely not

ObamaCare Simplified

Scenario B, shown below, contains one difference from scenario A.

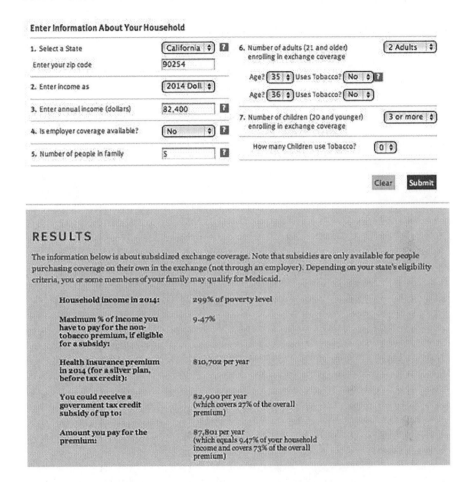

15. What is the difference between scenarios A and B?

    a. The state
    b. The number of children
    c. The number of dependents
    d. The income

16. How does this change affect the subsidy offered by the government?

    a. Increases the subsidy
    b. Decreases the subsidy
    c. No change

Now compare scenario B to scenario C, shown below.

Enter Information About Your Household

1. Select a State: California
   Enter your zip code: 90254
2. Enter income as: 2014 Doll
3. Enter annual income (dollars): 82,400
4. Is employer coverage available? No
5. Number of people in family: 5
6. Number of adults (21 and older) enrolling in exchange coverage: 2 Adults
   - Age: 35 Uses Tobacco? No
   - Age: 36 Uses Tobacco? No
7. Number of children (20 and younger) enrolling in exchange coverage: 3 or more
   - How many Children use Tobacco? 2

RESULTS

The information below is about subsidized exchange coverage. Note that subsidies are only available for people purchasing coverage on their own in the exchange (not through an employer). Depending on your state's eligibility criteria, you or some members of your family may qualify for Medicaid.

Household income in 2014:	299% of poverty level
Maximum % of income you have to pay for the non-tobacco premium, if eligible for a subsidy:	9.47% (before accounting for a tobacco surcharge, if applicable)
Health Insurance premium in 2014 (for a silver plan, before tax credit):	$10,702 per year In most states, insurers can charge a tobacco surcharge of up to 50% of your total premium before the tax credit. The tax credit cannot be applied to the tobacco surcharge.
You could receive a government tax credit subsidy of up to:	$2,900 per year (which covers 27% of the overall premium)
Amount you pay for the premium:	$7,801 per year (which equals 9.47% of your household income and covers 73% of the overall premium)

ObamaCare Simplified

17. What is the difference between scenarios B and C?

   a. The state
   b. The number of children
   c. The number of smokers
   d. The income

18. How does this change affect the subsidy offered by the government?

   a. Increases the subsidy
   b. Decreases the subsidy
   c. No change

Now compare scenario C to scenario D, shown below.

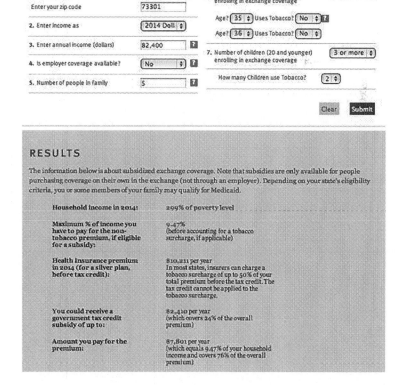

19. What is the difference between scenarios C and D?

    a. The state
    b. The number of children
    c. The number of smokers
    d. The income

20. How does this change affect the subsidy offered by the government?

    a. Increases the subsidy
    b. Decreases the subsidy
    c. No change

Answers

1. C. The main problem facing individuals searching for health insurance is affordability. People generally find premiums to be unaffordable. One reason for this is the paucity of competitors in the health insurance markets. The expansion of competition (with more insurers in the market) anticipated under ObamaCare is likely to trigger price rivalry and lower premium rates, increasing affordability. That is the fundamental premise of ObamaCare. Answers A and D do not mention the problem of affordability. Answer B is not correct because the problem is actually the opposite.

2. A. One prime reason for unaffordable rates is that there are too few competitors in the health insurance markets. Answer B is incorrect because the problem is the complete opposite. Choices C and D are incorrect because government regulation is part of the solution, and not the problem. This leaves choice A as the only correct answer.

3. D. Because they have fewer competitors, rural areas are likely to be hardest hit with high prices for health plans. Large cities have more businesses and bigger markets, while rural places tend to have fewer businesses and fewer choices. ObamaCare anticipates lower prices through competition and choices, so rural areas are at a disadvantage. Answers A and B are incorrect because urban and suburban areas enjoy an advantage in terms of competition, and choice C is incorrect because different rules apply to military families.

4. B. The correct answer is that hospitals are reluctant to lower prices for medical procedures, contending that these procedures are inherently costly for them. Answer A is incorrect because health insurance companies are concerned about the uncertainty of profits under ObamaCare.

5. A. High deductibles are prominent features of catastrophic plans. Other characteristics include low premiums and short-term hospital stays. Answers B, C, and D mistakenly contradict this.

6. D. Catastrophic plans are generally a good fit for people who do not have medical conditions and do not receive medical care or who cannot afford more coverage. Answers A, B, and C all mention characteristics that would require regular medical attention, and people with these conditions would not be good candidates for catastrophic health plans.

7. B. Catastrophic plans generally require individuals to pay for all medical costs up to a certain amount, usually several thousand dollars. After the deductible is met, costs for essential health benefits are generally paid by the plan. Most catastrophic plans cover three primary care visits per year at no cost (even before the deductible has been met) and also cover preventive services.

8. D. Catastrophic plans are perfect for people who want to ensure that they are covered in short emergencies. High deductibles are prominent features of these plans precisely because the plans are used in emergencies. Other characteristics include low premiums and coverage of short-term hospital stays. Answer A is incorrect because premiums are supposed to be lower. Choice B is incorrect because deductibles are supposed to be higher. Answer C is incorrect.

9. B. The answer is the Insurance Group A HMO plan. Since the prices are arranged in ascending order, the cheapest plan will be the first one on the list. The prices are located in the blue box on the right. All other answers refer to more expensive plans.

10. A. EPO stands for exclusive provider organization. This means that the insurance plan includes only health care providers within the network. The other three choices are fabricated.

11. B. Insurance Group B offers the cheapest non-HMO plan, the PPO catastrophic plan. Insurance Group C offers an EPO plan; however, it is the most expensive plan on the list. Insurance Group A offers only HMO plans. Therefore choice B is correct.

12. C. The question is answered in the information panel, which mentions the figure, 22 percent. This is the government subsidy a person in this situation might receive. Answer A is incorrect because it is the percentage of the poverty level rather than the subsidy percentage. Choices B and D are fabricated.

13. C. The screenshot above the results (question 7 in the drop-down menu) says that the applicant has "3 or more children (20 and younger)." Three is closest to the correct choice.

14. A. The household information panel (question 6 in the drop-down menu on the screenshot) says two adults will need insurance. This raises the strong possibility of a spouse. Answer A allows for this possibility. Answer B is wrong for ruling it out.

15. A. The only thing that changed between the two scenarios is the state. It changed from Florida to California. All the other choices are wrong because nothing else changed.

16. A. This change increased the subsidy, illustrating that the amount depends on the state of residence. That's because each state has the right to adopt its own version of federal policy. The subsidy increased from 22 percent to 27 percent of the premiums. It did not decrease or stay the same, making all the other choices incorrect.

17. C. The only thing that changed from scenario B to scenario C is the number of smokers. In scenario C, two of the children were smokers. Since all other characteristics stayed the same, answers A, B, and D are incorrect.

18. C. The correct answer is that there is no change. Although states can charge more for smokers, in California this does not make a difference. The subsidy was 27 percent in scenario B and 27 percent in scenario C.

19. A. The difference from scenario C to scenario D is the state. The state in scenario C is California while in scenario D it is Texas. Since nothing else changed, all the other answers are incorrect.

20. B. The correct answer is that there was a decrease in the subsidy offered from scenario C to scenario D.

Sources

Questions 1, 2, 3, 4: ABELSON, R., THOMAS, K., & McGINTY, J. (2013). *Health CareLaw Fails toLower Pricesfor Rural Areas. Nytimes.com*. Retrieved 13 December 2013, from http://www.nytimes.com/2013/10/24/business/health-law-fails-to-keep-prices-low-in-rural-areas.html?pagewanted=all&_r=0

Questions 5, 6, 7, 8: Ehealthinsurance.com,. *Catastrophic Health Insurance Plans - High Deductible Medical Plans*. Retrieved 15 December 2013, from http://www.ehealthinsurance.com/health-plans/catastrophic-insurance/

Questions 12, 13, 14, 15, 16, 17, 18, 19, 20: Kff.org,. *Subsidy Calculator*. Retrieved 16 December 2013, from http://kff.org/interactive/subsidy-calculator/

CHAPTER 9

How Does ObamaCare Affect Me?

Introduction to the chapter: The chapter addresses the philosophical and legislative origins of ObamaCare and its anticipated impact on economic activities in general and health care expenditures in particular.

Objective of the chapter: Once readers are familiar with the issues and solutions outlined in this chapter, they will understand the link between ObamaCare and future health care expenditures as well as employment in our nation. The analysis of health care costs in other industrialized countries versus those in the United States, and the composition of those costs, will show why regulation is needed to restrain such spending.

ObamaCare: the intersection of government, lawmaking, and justice

1. What is the ultimate goal of ObamaCare?

    a. To force health insurance on everyone
    b. To provide an equal opportunity for health insurance coverage
    c. To prevent private companies from selling health insurance
    d. To collect tax money

ObamaCare Simplified

2. Some people say, "It's not fair! The government cannot fine us for something we don't do!" What is the valid argument against this?

   a. The Commerce Clause in the Constitution states that the government can regulate commerce, including inactivity.
   b. The Commerce Clause in the Constitution states that the government can regulate activity in general.
   c. The power to levy taxes allows the government to tax inactivity.
   d. None of the above statements is true.

Economic implications: job creation, health care prices, and job loss

3. Will the new health care system create jobs?

   a. Yes
   b. No
   c. No way to know yet

4. Which of the following will be in high demand in the years to come due to ObamaCare?

   a. Nurse practitioners
   b. Engineers
   c. Dentists
   d. None of the above

5. Which of the following will be in high demand in the years to come due to ObamaCare?

   a. Plastic surgeons
   b. Computer programmers
   c. Business executives
   d. Any blue-collar worker

6. Overall, ObamaCare will lead to an increase in jobs in what field?

    a. Agriculture
    b. Industrial
    c. Service
    d. Equal growth in all three

7. Will the new health care system create unemployment?

    a. Not a chance
    b. Probably
    c. No way to know

8. How will ObamaCare affect the demand for physicians?

    a. Increase
    b. Decrease
    c. No change

9. ObamaCare will increase job opportunities for physician assistants and nurses but not for physicians.

    a. True
    b. False
    c. It is impossible to tell.

10. Although ObamaCare regulations have led some companies to cut work hours, people fail to realize that other job opportunities being created make up for this loss.

    a. True. ObamaCare is creating opportunities in the service sectors, such as human resources, information technology, and consulting.

b. True. There are more opportunities in lesser-known industries, such as logging, fishing, and mining, where there is a much higher demand than people realize.
c. False. There is no net gain or loss of jobs.
d. False. There is a net loss of jobs.

11. When will we know why there was an increase in part-time employment during the recession of 2007–09?

    a. Once ObamaCare takes complete effect
    b. We already know with certainty.
    c. It may be difficult to know with absolute certainty.

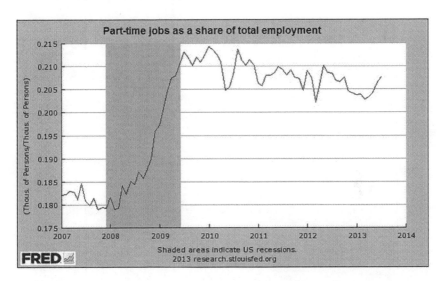

12. The graph above shows part-time jobs before, during, and after the recession. Which of the following percentages best describes the increase in part-time employment? (The shaded areas indicate the recession.)

    a. 1.5%
    b. 0.03%
    c. 3%
    d. 0.15%

13. The trend toward part-time employment after 2010 can best be described as what?

    a. Unchanging
    b. Decreasing
    c. Increasing
    d. It cannot be determined.

14. Evidence points to the recession, not ObamaCare, as the reason for an increase in part-time jobs.

    a. True, because the increase in part-time employment predates ObamaCare
    b. True, because the recession is more of a reason than ObamaCare for economic change
    c. True, because ObamaCare cannot affect the economy
    d. False, because the decrease in full-time employment came after ObamaCare was signed into law

Health care systems: other countries, historical results

15. Other countries do not spend as much as the United States does on medical care, yet they enjoy comparable or better health care. What is one of the main reasons for this?

    a. Medical procedures cost much more in the United States than in other countries.
    b. The US government pays for medical procedures for the underprivileged.
    c. Medicaid siphons money from the federal budget.
    d. There is no government regulation of health care.

16. Which country comes close to spending as much as the United States on health care?

    a. Japan
    b. Netherlands
    c. China
    d. New Zealand

17. Although the United States does not excel in health care, one area of medicine is the exception. Which is it?

    a. Orthopedic surgery and post-operative care
    b. Ophthalmology and Lasik surgery
    c. Cancer research and treatment
    d. Cardiology

18. Which medical procedures are more common in the United States compared to other developed countries?

    a. Cesarean sections (C-sections) and coronary bypass
    b. Coronary bypass and tonsillectomy
    c. Tonsillectomy and knee replacement
    d. Coronary bypass and knee replacement

19. Due to advances in technology, the cost of normal deliveries and cesarean sections is less in the U.S. compared to other developed countries such as Canada, Germany and Finland.

    a. True. The cost of obstetric procedures such as c-sections is lower in the U.S. than in other developed nations
    b. False. The cost of normal deliveries and c-sections is higher in the U.S. than in other developed nations
    c. False. The cost of obstetric procedures is comparable (little difference) across most developed nations

20. After examining what other countries have done, what is one solution to reduce excessive government spending?

    a. Regulate the cost of medical procedures.
    b. Stop spending on medical procedures and cut costs.
    c. No action is necessary; the costs will come down on their own.
    d. No action can reduce the cost of health care.

Answers

1. B. The overarching goal of ObamaCare is not to force everyone to have health insurance but to provide an equal opportunity for everyone to gain coverage. Answer A is incorrect because although the law strongly encourages individuals to have health insurance, the government will take no legal action against those who do not. Answer C is incorrect because private companies will be the main players in the health insurance market. Choice D is incorrect because although taxes are a source of revenue that will be generated through ObamaCare, they are not the law's main goal.

2. C. The government has the power to tax. The Commerce Clause, however, does not allow for regulation of inactivity, only activity. If you do not engage in commercial activity, you cannot be taxed. Answers A and B are incorrect because the Commerce Clause does not permit regulation of inactivity, and regulation of activity does not apply in this situation. Since answer C is correct, answer D is incorrect.

3. A. The new health care system will create jobs, particularly in the service sectors related to advising, consulting, and data entry, and among health care providers including doctors, nurse practitioners, and physician assistants. Malpractice lawyers and health care administrators may also gain jobs. Thus answer B is incorrect, and because we know and can predict this increase in job opportunities, choice C is also incorrect.

4. A. The new health care system will create jobs, as detailed in the previous answer. Choice B is incorrect because it does not specify a profession related specifically to health care. Answer C is not correct because the new health insurance system focuses on improvement of primary care in general rather than on a narrow field such as dental care. Since choice A is correct, choice D is incorrect.

5. B. The new health care system will create jobs, particularly in the service sectors related to advising, consulting, and data entry. Since the system will be geared more toward primary and preventive care, there will be a greater demand for physicians in those fields. Answer A is incorrect because plastic surgeons are not practitioners of primary or preventive care and will be unlikely to experience a surplus of demand. Answer B is correct because the tens of millions of newly insured people will create a data explosion, producing increased demand for IT personnel. Answer C is incorrect because it is not specifically relevant to health care. Choice D is incorrect because it is too general and encompasses all blue-collar employment. The service sector is the one expected to experience significant growth as a result of ObamaCare.

6. C. The new health care system will create jobs mostly in the service industry, and it is anticipated that more doctors, nurse practitioners, physician assistants, IT experts, and malpractice lawyers will be needed. All these careers are service-related. Answers A and B are incorrect because ObamaCare is not directly related to the agricultural or industrial sectors. Choice D is incorrect because ObamaCare does not affect all industries equally.

7. B. Since some companies are responding to ObamaCare policies by reducing employee hours, the law's negative repercussions could include job losses. Answer A is incorrect because it fails to examine this aspect of ObamaCare, which affects small and large businesses. Answer C is incorrect because it is possible to make an educated prediction about the law's impact on job loss.

8. A. The demand for physicians is high, and there is a shortage. Under ObamaCare, the demand for and use of primary and preventive care are expected to rise, increasing demand for physician services in those areas. Answer B is incorrect because health care demand is

expected to increase. Choice C is incorrect because we know that demand will increase.

9. B. As more people get insured, the demand for physicians will rise. There is and will be a high demand for physician assistants and nurses, and there will be a comparable need for physicians. Therefore choices A and C are incorrect.

10. A. The new health care system will create jobs, particularly in the service sectors related to advising, consulting, and data entry, and for doctors, nurse practitioners, and physician assistants. Since the system will be geared more toward primary care and preventive care, there will be a greater demand for physicians in those fields. Other job opportunities anticipated include those for malpractice lawyers and health care administrators. All of these careers are service-related. Answer B is incorrect because ObamaCare is not directly related to agricultural, mining, or other natural resource industries. Choices C and D are incorrect because there will most likely be an increase in job creation overall.

11. C. There is no way to be absolutely certain why there was a significant increase in part-time employment as a share of overall employment, but there are two theories. The first theory regarding the recession suggests the cause was purely economic. The other theory cites ObamaCare as the cause for the reduction in full-time employment. Answer A is incorrect because it is obvious that we will be better able to determine the cause once ObamaCare is fully in force. Answer B is incorrect because we do not know exactly why there was a decline in full-time employment. The chances are that we may never know, but we can use more data to hypothesize. This makes choice C the preferred answer.

12. C. The increase in part-time employment is shown as roughly from 0.180 to 0.210. That is a difference of 0.030, or 3 percent (0.03 times 100). Therefore answer C is correct.

13. B. Although the trend toward part-time employment after 2010 has not been as drastic as it was, the phenomenon continues. There has been about a 1 percent decrease overall. This makes choices A and C incorrect. Since the direction of the trend can be determined, answer D is also incorrect.

14. A. The correct answer is that the increase in part-time employment and the decrease in full-time employment started in 2009, while ObamaCare was not enacted until 2010. This supports the argument that the recession, not ObamaCare, was the cause. Answers B and C are incorrect because ObamaCare can affect the economy. Choice D is incorrect because the decrease in full-time employment occurred before ObamaCare was signed into law.

15. A. The main reason other countries have a similar or better quality of health care at much lower costs is the high expenditures related to medical procedures in the United States. Answer B is incorrect because the government does not directly pay for the indigent; the process is more complicated than that. Answer C is incorrect because Medicaid is not the root cause of the problem; rather, it is the high cost of medical procedures. Choice D is incorrect because there is some regulation of the health care industry in the United States (for instance, rules governing health insurance).

16. B. The Netherlands is right behind the United States in health care spending; still, it spends about a third less. Answer A is incorrect because Japan's annual health care expenditure is lower than the average for OECD countries. Answer C is incorrect because China is not even listed in the top thirty countries for health care expenditure despite its large population. Answer D is incorrect because although

New Zealand spends a significant amount on health care, it spends less than the Netherlands.

17. C. The United States has the world's best-quality care in cancer medicine, treatment, and research. All the other answers are incorrect because although the United States offers excellent care in those areas as well, compared with the amount spent and compared with other countries, the United States is at the top only in oncology and cancer research.

18. C. According to the Organization for Economic Co-operation and Development (OECD), the United States does more tonsillectomies and knee replacements than other developed countries. Answers A, B and D are incorrect.

19. B. The answer is False. Compared to other developed nations, the U.S. charges the most for normal deliveries and c-sections. In fact, a study conducted by OECD determined that obstetric procedures such as normal deliveries and c-sections cost nearly twice as much in the U.S. as in countries such as Canada, Germany or Finland.

20. A. Other countries reduce health care expenditures by regulating costs. An example is Japan where the government regulates prices to prevent rising costs in susceptible health care sectors. This policy keeps spending down while maintaining high standards of care. Answer B is incorrect because eliminating spending on medical procedures would lower the quality of health care. Choice C is incorrect because without regulation the costs might not come down. Answer D is incorrect because regulating prices can help reduce the cost of health care.

Sources

Questions 1, 2: YouTube,. (2012). *A Philosopher's Take on the Obamacare Decision*. Retrieved 13 December 2013, from http://www.youtube.com/watch?v=E-LT1vSkveQ

Questions 3, 4, 5, 6, 7: Wieczner, J. (2013). *10 careers boosted by Obamacare - MarketWatch. Marketwatch.com*. Retrieved 17 December 2013, from http://www.marketwatch.com/story/10-jobs-created-by-obamacare-2013-08-05

Questions 8: Senger, A. (2013). *Obamacare's Impact on Doctors—An Update. The Heritage Foundation*. Retrieved 17 December 2013, from http://www.heritage.org/research/reports/2013/08/obamacares-impact-on-doctors-an-update

Questions 9, 10: Hollander, C. (2013). *Obamacare Is Creating Jobs—Yes, Really. www.nationaljournal.com*. Retrieved 17 December 2013, from http://www.nationaljournal.com/magazine/obamacare-is-creating-jobs-yes-really-20130926

Questions 11, 12, 13, 14: Pethokoukis, J. (2013). *Are Obamacare opponents wrong about its impact on the US labor market -- or just early?. AEIdeas*. Retrieved 17 December 2013, from http://www.aei-ideas.org/2013/09/are-obamacare-opponents-wrong-about-its-impact-on-the-us-labor-market-or-just-early/

Questions 15, 16, 17, 18, 19, 20: PBS NewsHour,. (2013). *Health Costs: How the U.S. Compares With Other Countries | The Rundown | PBS NewsHour*. Retrieved 17 December 2013, from http://www.pbs.org/newshour/rundown/health-costs-how-the-us-compares-with-other-countries/

Question 18, 19: OECD Health Statistics. doi:10.1787/health-data-en

CHAPTER 10

ObamaCare as It Unfolds

Introduction to the chapter: As ObamaCare came into force, a number of issues, concerns, and challenges arose, triggering a variety of reactions. This chapter summarizes some of these events through simple scenarios that highlight lessons learned as we strive to attain affordable health care coverage for all.

Objective of the chapter: Many of the issues that confronted individuals seeking enrollment are presented here in the form of scenarios and questions to increase understanding. This chapter also covers socio-economic, logistic, and political factors that will affect the implementation, impact, and assessment of ObamaCare as it unfolds.

1. Some will gain subsidized health care, and others will make enough money to cover the costs themselves. But who will suffer the most under ObamaCare?

    a. Those below the poverty line
    b. Those at the poverty line
    c. The middle class
    d. Those whose income is more than four times the poverty level

2. What was one major problem facing the government and the people trying to access health insurance on the Internet marketplace?

   a. Low prices
   b. The majority of the population did not have access to the Internet.
   c. The website had technical problems.
   d. None of the above

3. If Sally had the same health plan for the last ten years, was she able to remain on it into 2014?

   a. Yes, definitely
   b. No, not necessarily
   c. It is impossible to determine this.

4. America spends approximately $3 trillion per year on health care. Which of the following statements is accurate?

   a. That is nothing compared with what other countries spend.
   b. America is one of the most cost-efficient countries when it comes to health care delivery.
   c. A fundamental problem is that 50 to 60 percent of that spending is wasteful.
   d. A fundamental problem is that 20 to 30 percent of that spending is wasteful.

5. Wasteful spending occurs for a variety of reasons. Which of the following statements about wasteful spending is true?

   a. Physicians are paid according to the number of services they deliver and not according to improvement in the health of their patients.
   b. Physicians are paid for every healthy patient.

c. The government does not spend $3 trillion on health care; rather, this amount represents the entire US gross domestic product.
d. The government offers its employees free health care.

6. What is defensive medicine?

   a. An approach to medicine that involves physicians avoiding high-risk situations
   b. Physicians working with patients to defend them against preventable diseases
   c. Nurses teaming up with physicians to see more patients
   d. None of the above

7. Why is defensive medicine driving up the cost of health care?

   a. Tailoring treatments to patients takes time and money in addition to reducing efficiency.
   b. Overtreatment exhausts limited resources and diverts funds from people who need them.
   c. Physicians and nurses are teaming up to do rounds, and the cost of seeing both at the same time is much higher than the cost of seeing one at a time.
   d. None of the above

8. Which of the following statements is true?

   a. Health insurance companies are offering prices comparable to those on the health exchange market.
   b. Health insurance companies are offering lower prices outside of the health exchange market.
   c. It depends on the health insurance company.
   d. None of the above

9. The prices of deductibles, premiums, and co-pays are higher than they were for a lot of people.

    a. True
    b. False
    c. There is not enough information to determine this.

10. Health care expenses account for how much of the US gross domestic product?

    a. Half
    b. One-third
    c. One-fourth
    d. One-fifth

11. Which of the following is not a reason for the persistent increase in health care costs?

    a. Medical technology
    b. Waste
    c. Unhealthy lifestyles
    d. None of the above

12. Which of the following is not a reason for the increase in health care costs?

    a. Provider prices
    b. Aging population
    c. Younger population and newly increased birthrate
    d. Taxes

13. Based on healthcare research, which field is experiencing the highest profit?

    a. Medical instrument and supply
    b. Major drug manufacturers
    c. Health insurance companies
    d. Medical appliance and equipment

14. Based on healthcare research, which field is experiencing a profit margin lower than expected?

    a. Medical instrument and supply
    b. Major drug manufacturers
    c. Health insurance companies
    d. Medical appliance and equipment

15. What percentage of Americans lost their health insurance when ObamaCare was implemented in October 2013 despite assurances that they would not lose their coverage?

    a. 5%
    b. 10%
    c. 15%
    d. none

16. If Jim has a son who turns twenty-seven this month, will his son need to sign up for his own insurance?

    a. Yes
    b. No
    c. Eventually, but not until the next open enrollment period

17. Can people enroll for health insurance outside of the open enrollment dates?

    a. Yes
    b. No
    c. Only if they have a "life-changing" event

18. Which of the following qualify as "life-changing events"?

    a. Having a child
    b. Losing a job
    c. Moving within the same state
    d. More than one of the above

19. By when did consumers have to pay for their coverage to be insured by January 2014?

    a. January 1, 2014
    b. December 1, 2013
    c. November 15, 2013
    d. Generally by December 15, 2013, but it depended on the state

20. What two characteristics do health insurance companies use to determine premiums?

    a. Two of the worst pre-existing health conditions
    b. Family health history and state of residence
    c. Name and state residence
    d. Age and state residence

Answers

1. C. The correct answer is those who do not qualify for subsidies but still have to purchase insurance despite modest income. Answers A and B are incorrect because those below or at the poverty line get subsidized health insurance or are not required to purchase coverage. Answer D is incorrect because those with income at four times the poverty level should have sufficient money to pay for health insurance.

2. C. People trying to purchase health insurance on the Internet marketplace faced technical problems associated with the website. Initially, this prevented many people from signing up for coverage. Answer A is incorrect because people would welcome low-price health insurance. Choice B is incorrect because according to the *Washington Post*, almost 85 percent of Americans had Internet access. Since the correct answer is C, choice D is incorrect.

3. B. The correct answer is no. If the plan did not meet the minimum requirements, Sally could not remain on it. Answer A is incorrect because it directly contradicts the correct answer. Since it is possible to determine the status of Sally's insurance plan, choice C is incorrect.

4. D. A major problem is that 20 to 30 percent of US health care spending is wasteful. Answer A is incorrect because the United States spends more on health care than any other country. Answer B is incorrect because despite the costs, the United States does not deliver the best health care. This means that America does not have one of the most cost-effective health care systems. Choice C is incorrect because the range of 50 to 60 percent is too high.

5. A. The health care system pays physicians according to the number of services they deliver as opposed to the health of their patients. This approach is known as a fee-for-service system. Answer B is

incorrect because physicians are not paid based on the health of their patients. Answer C is incorrect because the figure $3 trillion refers to US health care expenditures and not to the US GDP. Choice D is incorrect because health care is not free; the expense must be paid by some means.

6. A. Doctors practicing defensive medicine avoid situations that may cause litigation. Lawsuits arise most often with high-risk patients; therefore, defensive medicine entails avoiding high-risk medical conditions. Answer B is incorrect because it describes preventive rather than defensive medicine. Answer C is incorrect because when nurses team up with physicians to improve patient care, they are practicing collaborative medicine, not defensive medicine. Choice D is incorrect.

7. B. Defensive medicine involves conducting myriad unnecessary medical procedures and tests to reduce liability. Answers A and C are incorrect because collaborative treatment is not defensive medicine, and indeed the approach yields efficiency. Answer B is correct because it accurately explains how defensive medicine drives up health care expenditures through overtreatment and diversion of resources needed elsewhere.

8. A. The health exchange market is becoming competitive, and as of 2013, the exchange market prices were comparable to those offered by insurance companies operating outside of the exchange. Answer B is incorrect because insurance companies cannot afford to discount policy prices, limiting their profits without any clear advantage. Answer C is incorrect because the nature or philosophy of a health insurance company isn't a significant factor in a competitive market with relatively stable prices. Since A is the correct answer, choice D is incorrect.

ObamaCare Simplified

9. A. The prices insurance companies offer on the health exchange markets are higher than before ObamaCare was implemented. This is so for a number of reasons including the fact that many plans did not have all of the components that ObamaCare requires. Answer C is incorrect because many people have reported that their premiums and deductibles increased, and so there is a way to determine this. Choice B is incorrect because the statement is true.

10. D. The correct answer is about one fifth. Choices A, B, and C are too high. The amount is fairly large compared with the figures in other countries.

11. D. The correct answer is "None of the above" because all the statements are reasons for the increased cost of health care. Answer A is incorrect because when hospitals buy technology, patients are charged more to recover technology investment costs. Choice B is incorrect because a large amount of waste yields more cost and less production. Answer C is incorrect because unhealthy lifestyles lead to more doctor's visits and higher costs for health care.

12. C. The correct answer is a younger population and a newly increased birthrate. These factors would not increase the cost of health care. Choice A is incorrect because higher provider prices increase the amount spent on health care. Choice B is incorrect because older people require more medical attention and this means more bills for geriatric services. Answer D is incorrect because taxes increase the prices of goods and services including health care.

13. B. According to a 2012 Yahoo finance report, major drug manufacturers have the highest profit margin, followed by medical appliance and equipment and medical instrument and supply.

14. C. Health insurance companies have a lower profit margin than anticipated. They were expected to receive an influx of customers,

but because of administrative problems this didn't happen. This reduced their profit margin.

15. A. According to the *Washington Post*, 5 percent of policyholders lost their plans because of ObamaCare. Thus answer D is incorrect. Answers B and C are incorrect because the numbers are too high.

16. A. The correct answer is that Jim will have to get his own insurance policy. That's because turning twenty-seven counts as a life-changing event. Life-changing events qualify individuals to sign up for insurance outside of the dates for open enrollment. Answer B is incorrect because Jim will be allowed to sign up for insurance. Choice C is incorrect because he qualifies under the "life-changing event" clause. Examples of life-changing events include moving away from your parents, getting married or divorced, and having children.

17. C. The correct answer is that people can sign up for insurance outside of the open enrollment dates only if they qualify. Life-changing events qualify individuals to do this. Choice A is incorrect because it does not indicate the requirement for a life-changing event. Answer B is incorrect because people can apply outside of the open enrollment dates. These are typical dates for open enrollment: 2014 open enrollment ends on March 31, 2014; 2015 open enrollment starts November 15, 2014, and 2015 open enrollment ends February 15, 2015. These dates may, however, change.

18. D. "More than one of the above" is the correct choice. Answer A is correct because having a child increases the number of household members, affecting the economic percentile that goes into calculating a premium; this counts as a life-changing event. Losing a job also qualifies as a life-changing event because it affects total income, which is also used to determine subsidies and premiums. Answer C is not a life-changing event because it is within the same state. However, moving outside of the state in which the insurance

was purchased qualifies as a life-changing event because states have different insurance policies.

19. D. December 15 was the initial deadline for consumers to pay the premiums for their health insurance policies, although modifications were made. Answers B and C are too early to be correct for most states, and choice A is too late for most states.

20. D. Answers A and B are incorrect because ObamaCare does not allow pre-existing conditions to affect insurance premiums. Answer C is incorrect because a name has nothing to do with health status. The correct answer is age and state of residence.

Sources

Questions 1, 2, 3: Eunjuna Cha, A., & Sun, L. (2013). *For consumers whose health premiums will go up under new law, sticker shock leads to anger*. Washington Post. Retrieved 17 December 2013, from http://www.washingtonpost.com/national/health-science/for-consumers-whose-health-premiums-will-go-up-under-new-law-sticker-shock-leads-to-anger/2013/11/03/d858dd28-44a9-11e3-b6f8-3782ff6cb769_story.html

Questions 4 and 5: *National Health Expenditures, 2012 Highlights*. (2012). Retrieved 30 November 2013, from http://www.cms.gov/Research-Statistics-Data-and-Systems/Statistics-Trends-and-Reports/NationalHealthExpendData/downloads/proj2012.pdf

Questions 4, 5, 6, 7: Ahip.org,. *America's Health Insurance Plans - Rising Health Care Costs*. Retrieved 30 November 2013, from http://www.ahip.org/Issues/Rising-Health-Care-Costs.aspx

Questions 8,9: Los Angeles Times Articles,. (2011). *What to expect from company health insurance plans in 2014*. Retrieved 30 November 2013, from http://articles.latimes.com/2013/nov/03/business/la-fi-employee-insurance-20131103

Questions 10, 11, 12, 13, 14: Aetna.com,. (2013). *The Facts About Rising Health Care Costs*. Retrieved 30 November 2013, from http://www.aetna.com/health-reform-connection/aetnas-vision/facts-about-costs.html

Question 15: Eilperin, J. (2013). *President Obama apologizes to Americans who are losing their health insurance*. Washington Post. Retrieved 30 November 2013, from http://www.washingtonpost.com/politics/president-obama-apologizes-to-americans-who-are-losing-their-health-insurance/2013/11/07/2306818e-4803-11e3-a196-3544a03c2351_story.html

Questions 16, 17, 18, 19, 20: Washington Post,. *All your Obamacare questions answered*. Retrieved 30 November 2013, from http://apps.washingtonpost.com/g/page/politics/all-your-obamacare-questions-answered/564/

CHAPTER 11

ObamaCare Literacy in Medical Technology

Introduction to the chapter: This chapter is an introduction to the field of medical technology, an important part of the health care market. Those interested in medical technology will find the chapter a useful starting point in their journey toward literacy in this area.

Objective of the chapter: The goal of this chapter is to familiarize readers with common devices used in medical procedures, how they are regulated, and who does the regulation. The chapter touches on the connection between ObamaCare and the tax on medical devices. There is also a section on the administrative procedures involved in recalling already approved medical devices.

Medical Technology

1. Which government agency decides whether a medical device is taxable?

    a. Food and Drug Administration (FDA)
    b. Bureau of Medical Technology and Research
    c. Department of Public Health
    d. Internal Revenue Service

2. How is a medical device defined?

    a. Any technology that is involved in collecting information about body systems
    b. Any technology used on humans that does not involve chemical reactions and is not metabolized in humans and that has the purpose of diagnosis, treatment, or prevention of disease or other conditions
    c. Select technologies most commonly used in hospital settings
    d. Technology that is used in any medical context and that costs more than $1,000

3. What medical devices are commonly used in hospitals?

    a. CT scanners
    b. Stents
    c. Defibrillators
    d. All of the above

4. Which medical device is not commonly used in hospitals?

    a. Stethoscope
    b. X-ray machine
    c. Electrocardiogram
    d. Personal diagnosis robotics

5. The debate over what is considered a medical device revolves around a definition of the term. Some people believe that devices should not be taxed unless they are directly used to diagnose, treat, or monitor the patient. Which of the following "devices" would such a definition affect with respect to taxation?

    a. Stethoscopes
    b. Defibrillators

c. Software
d. Tongue depressors

6. Medical devices represent a crucial improvement in the medical field because they allow for quicker and more precise diagnoses. As some medical devices are becoming cheaper and more readily available, a question arises. Are prescriptions required for their purchase?

    a. Yes
    b. No
    c. It depends on the type of equipment.
    d. The issue has not yet been decided.

7. If a prescription is required, who is certified to prescribe a medical device?

    a. It is impossible to know because the question has not yet been decided.
    b. This question is irrelevant because a prescription is not required for any medical device.
    c. Any physician.
    d. It depends on the law at the state level.

8. If Sam wants to know whether an item is considered a medical device, where should he look for information?

    a. The FDA online database
    b. He would have to contact a doctor's office and ask to speak with the technology manager.
    c. The list of medical devices has not yet been compiled.
    d. Sam will not be able to access that information unless he submits a form to the FDA demonstrating a need for it.

9. In some instances, FDA-approved medical devices pose a risk greater than initial assessments showed. If this is the case after a device has been on the market for some time, what action will the FDA have to take?

   a. Reclaim
   b. Recall
   c. Collection
   d. No action; there is no provision for this situation.

10. Complications can arise when a medical device that is being recalled has been implanted in a patient. Which of the following should the patient do?

    a. Schedule an emergency surgical procedure to remove the implant independent of a physician consultation
    b. Ignore the recall as long as he/she feels well
    c. Schedule an appointment with a physician
    d. None of the above

11. While the use of technology in medicine has benefits, which of the following is an important and recognized negative repercussion?

    a. Technology abuse (indiscriminate use of technology)
    b. Contamination of devices due to human error
    c. Technology is too cheap to use.
    d. There are no negative repercussions.

12. Which of the following is a negative repercussion of technology?

    a. Possible exposure to radiation
    b. Technology allows us to be more efficient.
    c. Technology reduces efficiency by necessitating the employment of specialized technicians.
    d. None of the above

13. Which of the following is a reasonable solution to the high costs associated with the use of medical technology?

    a. Use technology more until the price is brought down.
    b. There is no reasonable solution to the high costs associated with technology.
    c. Limit the use of technology to a need-only basis.
    d. Stop using technology until it is made cheaper.

14. Which of the following is a reasonable solution to the high costs associated with the use of medical technology?

    a. Examine laws that govern pricing of technology on the markets.
    b. Examine ways in which technology is being used indiscriminately.
    c. Examine wasteful expenditures related to employee salaries.
    d. Boycott technology altogether.

15. What are excluded services?

    a. Services that a certain doctor cannot perform
    b. Services that are not considered medically necessary
    c. Services that are not covered by an individual's health plan
    d. None of the above

The chart below shows data as of July 2013.

Rank	Medical Services	% of Health Plans Excluding Service
1	Long-term Care	98%
2	Cosmetic Surgery	98%
3	Infertility Treatment	94%
4	Weight Loss Program	93%
5	Private Nursing	92%
6	Acupuncture	92%
7	Children's Dental Check-up	92%
8	Weight Loss Surgery	90%
9	Children's Eye glasses	87%
10	Adult Dental Services	81%

Adapted from HealthPocket: http://www.healthpocket.com/healthcare-research/infostat/top-10-medical-services-excluded-by-health-insurance

16. Which of the following medical services/procedures was least often covered by insurance plans?

   a. Breast implants
   b. Braces
   c. Weight loss treatment
   d. In-vitro fertilization

17. What percentage of health plans excluded children's dental checkups?

   a. 70%
   b. 80%
   c. 90%
   d. It is impossible to tell because the percentage is not on the chart.

18. Weight loss programs and weight loss surgery are becoming common medical procedures, but they are not typically covered by insurance companies. Under the Affordable Care Act, the pre-existing condition of obesity can prevent someone from receiving a medical plan until 2014. Which of the following is correct regarding that statement?

    a. The statement is not true because under ObamaCare, health insurance companies cannot deny insurance based on any pre-existing condition.
    b. The statement is true.
    c. There is not enough information to answer this question.

19. Which of the following is an advance in medical information technology?

    a. More physicians are using electronic medical records.
    b. Fewer physicians are relying on electronic medical records.
    c. There is little research on the subject.
    d. There are no advances in medical information technology.

20. Which of the following is not a positive consequence of better medical information technology?

    a. Younger doctors will be attracted to medical information technology.
    b. A compilation of data represents a single target for hackers.
    c. The cost of information management will be brought down.
    d. Service jobs in the IT sector will increase.

Answers

1. A. The FDA regulates medical technology in addition to food and drugs. The Bureau of Medical Technology was fabricated, and the Department of Public Health is not responsible for medical technology. The Internal Revenue Service is not responsible for deciding whether something is taxed, it only collect the taxes imposed on the devices.

2. B. The FDA defines a medical device as one that is not metabolized or chemically reactive to achieve its purpose. Answer A, "technology for collecting information," is incorrect because it is too vague and because medical devices can have purposes beyond collecting information. Similarly, choice C is not correct because medical devices are not limited to a specific list. Answer D includes an incorrect definition. The definition of a medical device is not determined by price.

3. D. All of the above are medical devices commonly used in hospitals. CT scanners are used for imaging of internal organs; stents are small mesh tubes used to treat narrow or weak arteries; defibrillators are used for resuscitation if the heart stops functioning properly.

4. D. Personal diagnosis robots are machines that monitor patient status and other patient information to diagnose diseases. This technology is not yet widely used and is still in progress. Answers A, B, and C, however, are commonly used in the hospital setting. This makes the correct answer D.

5. C. This question excludes from the definition of medical technology technologies that do not come into direct contact with the patient. Software is an example of a medical device that does not directly treat patients, and so taxation may change for that. The other devices

are used in direct contact with patients and would not be the correct answer to the question.

6. C. Some medical devices require prescriptions for purchase while others do not. It depends on the type of equipment. Answers A and B are too definite to be correct, and choice D is incorrect because it says that the FDA has not yet decided.

7. D. The correct answer is that it depends on the law at the state level. Answer C is incorrect because physicians are not always the only professionals authorized to prescribe medical devices. Optometrists, for example, are not physicians but could prescribe certain visual devices. Answer A is incorrect because the question has been decided. Answer B is incorrect because medical devices such as contact lenses do require prescriptions.

8. A. The FDA provides an online database of medical devices that are taxed. Answers B and D are unnecessarily complicated procedures that may or may not answer Sam's question, and choice C is incorrect because the FDA keeps an updated list on its website.

9. B. A recall is in force when a good is deemed unfit for consumption after it has been made available. Answers A and C are incorrect terms for this definition. Answer D is incorrect because there is a provision that addresses this situation.

10. C. This is the correct answer because a patient must see a physician to determine what action should be taken to rectify the situation. Answer A is incorrect because implants complicate recalls, and a physician consultation is needed to discuss what, if anything, must be done. Answer B is incorrect because all recalls should be taken

seriously, and a patient should schedule an appointment with a physician as soon as possible. Choice D is incorrect.

11. A. Abuse has been a major negative repercussion of technology, which is expensive and should be used only when needed. Answer B is incorrect because it refers to humans and not to technology. Choice C is incorrect because technology is not necessarily cheap. Answer D is incorrect because there are negative repercussions.

12. A. Possible exposure to radiation is a negative repercussion because radiation, though helpful in scanning body tissues, can damage cells and have long-term side effects. Answer B is incorrect because an increase in efficiency is not a negative repercussion. Answer C is incorrect because technology does not reduce efficiency. Choice D is incorrect because answer A is correct.

13. C. A conservative or controlled use of technology can reduce costs until technology is cheaper. Answer A is incorrect because frequent use of expensive technology will not necessarily curtail the price. Answer B is incorrect because there is a reasonable way to deal with the high costs. Choice D is incorrect because technology is used to make treatment of some diseases feasible, and stopping the use of technology in such cases could be unethical and unwarranted.

14. B. The high price of medical technology could be reduced by curtailing costs related to indiscriminate use of this technology. Answer A is incorrect because the pricing of technology is not necessarily the problem: certain costs must be met with every technological device. Answer C is incorrect because employee salaries are not where

money is being wasted. Choice D is incorrect because abandoning technology use means refusing to accept improvement to our lives.

15. C. Excluded services are procedures or services that are not covered by health insurance plans. Answers A and B give incorrect definitions. Answer D is incorrect.

16. A. Examining the chart helps answer this question. The higher the ranking of a service the less likely it is to be covered by health insurance plans. The service highest on the chart is cosmetic surgery. Cosmetic breast implants are in this category, making this the least-covered service. Answers B, C, and D are incorrect because they are further down the chart.

17. C. Looking at the chart can help solve this question. Children's dental checkups were excluded by 92 percent of health plans. The closest answer is C. Answers A and B are incorrect because the percentages are too low. Choice D is incorrect because "children's dental checkups" is on the chart.

18. B. The correct answer is that as of July 2013 obesity was not considered a disease or a pre-existing condition. Whether obesity is such a condition remains under debate. Some insurance companies consider it so, while others don't. Answer A is incorrect because at the time of the measured statistics, the statement was true. It is still true in some cases, but obesity is accepted by many (including the American Medical Association) as a disease and a pre-existing condition. Answer C is incorrect because there is no missing information.

19. A. More physicians are using electronic medical records, and this could eventually help make a central database feasible. Answer B is incorrect because more physicians are using and keeping electronic medical records. Choice C is incorrect because a great deal of

research is being done on medical information technology. Answer D is incorrect because there has been improvement in this technology.

20. B. The compilation of people's medical records will make data more accessible for hackers unless more stringent security measures are taken. Answers A, B, and C are incorrect because they are positive consequences.

Sources

Questions 1, 2, 3, 4, 5: Federalregister.gov,. (2012). *Federal Register | Taxable Medical Devices*. Retrieved 10 January 2014, from https://www.federalregister.gov/articles/2012/12/07/2012-29628/taxable-medical-devices

Questions 6, 7, 8, 9, 10: Fda.gov,. (2014). *Medical Devices*. Retrieved 10 January 2014, from http://www.fda.gov/AboutFDA/Transparency/Basics/ucm193731.htm

Questions 11, 12, 13, 14: Ncbi.nlm.nih.gov,. (1990). *Ethical problems of medical technol... [Bull Pan Am Health Organ. 1990] - PubMed - NCBI*. Retrieved 10 January 2014, from http://www.ncbi.nlm.nih.gov/pubmed/2073552

Questions 16, 17, 18: Healthpocket.com,. (2013). *Top 10 Healthcare Services Excluded Under Obamacare - Healthpocket*. Retrieved 12 January 2014, from https://www.healthpocket.com/healthcare-research/infostat/top-10-excluded-services-obamacare#.VBm1nBaQIEM

Questions 15: Webteam, U. (2014). *Glossary of Health Coverage and Medical Terms | Human Resources | University of Pittsburgh. Hr.pitt.edu*. Retrieved 12 January 2014, from http://www.hr.pitt.edu/benefits/student-be/Glossary

Questions 19, 20: Cutler, D. (2013). *Why Medicine Will Be More Like Walmart | MIT Technology Review. MIT Technology Review*. Retrieved 11 January 2014, from http://www.technologyreview.com/news/518906/why-medicine-will-be-more-like-walmart/

Made in the USA
Lexington, KY
03 January 2015